THE INNER BONDING MASTERCLASS

Books by Margaret Paul

Do I Have To Give Up Me To Be Loved By You?
With Dr. Jordan Paul

*Do I Have To Give Up Me To Be Loved By You? . . .
The Workbook*
With Dr. Jordan Paul

Do I Have To Give Up Me To Be Loved By My Kids?
With Dr. Jordan Paul and Bonnie B. Hesse

Healing Your Aloneness
With Dr. Erika Chopich

The Healing Your Aloneness Workbook
With Dr. Erika Chopich

Inner Bonding

*Diet For Divine Connection: Beyond Junk Food and
Junk Thoughts to At-Will Divine Connection*

*The Inner Bonding Workbook: Six Steps to Healing Yourself
and Connecting With Your Divine guidance*

*6-Steps to Total Self-Healing:
The Inner Bonding Process*

*How to Become Strong Enough to Love:
Creating Loving Relationships Through
the Six-Step Pathway of Inner Bonding*

Lonely No More
With Dr. Erika Chopich

THE INNER BONDING MASTERCLASS

MARGARET PAUL, PhD

Published 2025 by Gildan Media LLC
aka G&D Media
www.GandDmedia.com

INNER BONDING MASTERCLASS. Copyright ©2025 by Margaret Paul, PhD, and Inner Bonding®. All rights reserved.

No part of this book may be used, reproduced or transmitted in any manner whatsoever, by any means (electronic, photocopying, recording, or otherwise), without the prior written permission of the author, except in the case of brief quotations embodied in critical articles and reviews. No liability is assumed with respect to the use of the information contained within. Although every precaution has been taken, the author and publisher assume no liability for errors or omissions. Neither is any liability assumed for damages resulting from the use of the information contained herein.

Front cover design by David Rheinhardt of Pyrographx

Interior design by Meghan Day Healey of Story Horse, LLC

Library of Congress Cataloging-in-Publication Data is available upon request

ISBN: 978-1-7225-0691-9

10   9   8   7   6   5   4   3   2   1

Contents

    Introduction.................................... 7
1 The Six Steps of Inner Bonding.................. 9
2 Speaking Up for Yourself 21
3 Gaining Emotional Freedom..................... 31
4 Relationship Systems.......................... 37
5 Overcoming Resistance 45
6 Fear and Courage............................. 53
7 Remaining Happy Among Unhappy People..... 63
8 Healing the Fear of Rejection.................. 71
9 Welcoming Your Sensitivity 81
10 How to Avoid Being a Scapegoat............... 87
11 Healing from the Mother Wound................ 97

Contents

12 How to Stop Feeling Like a Victim 107

13 Overcoming Rumination 115

14 Previous Trauma and Personal Strength 123

15 Communication in Relationships 129

16 Healing from an Abusive Relationship. 137

17 Moving Past Social Phobia. 145

18 Feeling Your Feelings. 151

19 Staying Centered. 159

20 Healing Addictions 171

    Epilogue. 179

    About the Author. 181

Introduction

I'm excited to offer you this peek into my biweekly masterclass, which is the result of my lifetime of personal inner work and of over fifty-five years of work with clients. Over these many years, Inner Bonding has become a powerful life-changing process for healing self-abandonment and for learning to love and value yourself. Inner Bonding is a comprehensive and practical six-step self-healing process that always works when you do it.

While Inner Bonding has been proven to help hundreds of thousands of people all over the world in their healing journey, I have found that some people still have questions about the process that are unique to their situation. Perhaps you went through a divorce recently and you feel lost, or you have trouble saying no to people, or you don't know what to do when someone blames you for something, or how to manage flashbacks from the past that are affecting your current life, and you're unsure of how to deal with it or how Inner Bonding can help.

To address this and many other issues, I've created my Inner Bonding Masterclass to provide my own inspirational mentoring, guided meditations, and laser coaching so that you can practice Inner Bonding more effectively and apply it to your life.

Just imagine rapidly discovering subconscious or unconscious false beliefs about yourself, others, and your higher power that are limiting you, and being able to rapidly heal these limiting beliefs, as well as healing guilt, shame, anxiety, depression, anger, jealousy, emptiness, and aloneness. This masterclass helps you move beyond self-judgment into self-compassion where you can address the resistance that may be keeping you stuck. You will learn from people who are healing their self-abandonment, healing their relationship conflicts, attaining the intimacy they've always wanted, and learning how to share love rather than always trying to get love.

In this book, you'll learn all this and more. Dialogues with Inner Bonding Masterclass participants are included to address specific issues that may apply to your life. Names have been changed to protect confidentiality.

I love doing this biweekly masterclass. I love that I can quickly see the underlying issue in the laser sessions I do with people and offer them the way to healing. I love seeing the progress that people make through the masterclass.

I hope that you not only benefit from this book, but that you join my Inner Bonding Masterclass and experience live the incredible power of Inner Bonding.

1

The Six Steps of Inner Bonding

As you'll see throughout this book, Inner Bonding is a process containing six steps. This masterclass will go into these steps in great detail, but here they are, for quick reference:

1. Be willing to feel pain and/or fear, and take responsibility for your feelings and security.
2. Choose the intent to learn about love and fear. Invite spirit into your heart. Open your heart to compassion and become a loving adult.
3. Welcome and dialogue with your core soul self—your inner child—and wounded self, exploring fears, false beliefs, memories, and resulting behavior that is causing the pain. Explore gifts and what brings joy to your inner child.
4. Dialogue with spiritual guidance, exploring truth and loving action toward your inner child.
5. Take loving action. Put God into motion.
6. Evaluate the effectiveness of your actions.

An Inner Bonding Meditation

Here is a meditation to give you a taste of the Inner Bonding process, indicating each step. You can work with it in several ways:
1. Read this book and do the meditation step by step as you read.
2. Have a friend read the meditation aloud and follow the spoken directions step by step.
3. Record the meditation in your own voice and play it back to yourself as you go through the exercise.
4. Use my instructions in the audio counterpart to this work: *The Inner Bonding Masterclass* (in three volumes).

When you are listening to audio instructions, you can stop at any time to give yourself as much time as you need with each step. If you are having a friend read to you, you can ask them to stop as you process the material that comes up.

Here is the meditation: Take a couple of deep breaths and put your mind on your breath. Follow your breath as it takes you in and out of your body and let it take you deeper inside. As you go in, scan your body for any physical sensations, because our emotions often show up as physical sensations. As you're breathing in, you're scanning your body to notice any tightness, tension, numbness, fluttering, excitement, or any other feeling. Just notice what comes up: Move toward it. Welcome it. Welcome all feelings as information, being with your feelings, embracing them, and deciding that you want to learn to take responsibility for them and learn about what they are telling you. (This is **step one**.)

Breathe into your heart, opening to learning about how you're treating yourself, what you're telling yourself that may be causing anything less than peace and fullness inside, what you're doing or not doing, and about any false beliefs that you need to become aware of.

Breathing that in and visualizing your higher guidance, whatever that is for you. If you're not in touch with a source of higher guidance, visualize an older, wiser part of you. Invite the love, compassion, strength, wisdom, courage, and truth of that higher source of love and truth into your heart just by saying to yourself, "I invite your love and your compassion, your strength, and your wisdom, and your courage and your truth into my heart."

Spirit is always here, just waiting for an invitation from us, but it doesn't come in by itself. We have to be open. We have to invite it in. That's what you're doing right now, inviting love, compassion, strength, wisdom, courage, and truth into your heart, and breathing it in. (This is **step two**.)

Now go down inside to whatever the feelings are. If there's anything less than peace and fullness inside, that's your soul—your inner child—communicating with you. Ask what you're doing or not doing, what you're telling yourself, and how you're treating yourself that may be causing a painful emotion. If you're feeling loneliness, heartbreak, grief, helplessness, or sorrow, go in and see what is happening externally that may be causing those existential feelings of life. If you are treating yourself in some way that brings about the wounded feelings of anxiety, depression, guilt, shame, emptiness, aloneness, anger, resentment, jealousy, envy, and so on, let your inner child speak to you about what you're doing. Let the answers come from inside, not from your mind. Let that feeling speak to you about how you are treating yourself that is causing these feelings.

Then go a little deeper. Go into the wounded part of you, the part that's filled with fear and false beliefs. You want to go down in there, because that's where you uncover false beliefs that you might not be aware of. Maybe you're pressuring yourself in some way that's causing anxiety. Maybe you're ignoring your feelings that may be causing depression. Maybe you're telling yourself you've got to be perfect, you've got to do everything right, or you'd better not make a mistake, or you better not fail.

Or you might be coming from core false beliefs such as "I'm not worthy" or "I'm not lovable" or "I'm not good enough." Are you treating yourself in ways you were treated or ways your parents or other caregivers treated themselves? There are many ways we treat ourselves that cause distress.

Go inside now and see what you discover there. You can take as much time as you want. This is how you discover subconscious or unconscious false beliefs. (This is **step three**.)

Then we go to **step four**. Now imagine yourself in a very beautiful place in nature, sitting at a picnic table or on a blanket or on a bank by a river, with your higher self, your older, wiser self. It can be an angel, a teacher, Jesus, Buddha, or Mother Mary—whatever works for you. Now ask your higher guidance what the truth is about any false beliefs you've discovered.

You might feel that you're just making up whatever comes through, or nothing might come through. That's okay. If you keep asking with an intent to learn, you will eventually receive an answer, and over time and practice, you will learn to trust the information coming from your guidance.

Now ask your guidance, what's loving to me? What's loving to my inner child? What is in my highest good? What would a loving adult do? How do I need to be treating myself that would make my soul, my inner child, feel safe and loved and important? Again, you might not get an answer right away, but with practice, it becomes easier and easier to get that information about truth and love.

If the answer is something you can do right now, do it. If not, imagine doing it. Imagine being loving to yourself. Imagine taking a loving action, holding out yourself, speaking up for yourself, reaching out for help, whatever the loving action would be. Imagine doing it, which is **step five** of Inner Bonding. Then imagine how you would feel if you were actually taking a loving action for yourself. That's **step six** of Inner Bonding.

My hope is that you will start to practice these steps, because they're powerful. The more you practice them, the more you will develop new neural pathways in your higher brain for the loving adult. The wounded self is in the lower left brain. It's programmed to repeat itself, like a broken record. These programmed false beliefs, repeated over and over, will limit you cause they cause you pain. By practicing Inner Bonding and developing your spiritually connected loving adult, you can powerfully change your life toward so much more inner peace and joy,

Parts of the Self

To understand the Inner Bonding process, it's necessary to understand the different parts of ourselves.

First is our *inner child*, our soul, which is in the lower right brain. Our inner child needs nurturing and loving actions by our loving adult.

Next is the *wounded self*, which lies in the lower left part of the brain. This part holds the painful experiences and traumas of the past, and the false beliefs and self-abandoning behavior that result. Our wounded self can be many different ages, depending on when we absorbed a false belief.

In the upper left brain is the *male aspect* of the *loving adult*, which is the part of us that takes action. The actions we take are either informed by our lower left brain, our wounded self, or by our upper right brain, *the feminine aspect of the loving adult*. (We all have masculine and feminine aspects in us.)

Our upper right brain is born with the ability to connect with our *higher self* or *higher guidance*. So when our actions are governed by our upper right brain, they are governed by love, and when they are governed by our lower left brain, they are governed by fear and false beliefs.

PARTS OF THE SELF
1. Inner child, true soul self (lower right brain)
2. Wounded self, (lower left brain)

3. Loving adult (both sides of the higher brain)
4. Higher self

Many of us don't connect with our higher self: We let the wounded self inform us. Actions informed by our lower left brain are not loving to ourselves or others. But when our actions are being informed by our upper right brain, connecting to spirit, they are loving to ourselves, others, animals, and the planet.

We need to learn to do what we came here to do, which is to evolve in our ability to love and express our gifts on the planet. We do this by learning to connect with and nurture the inner child, to set limits on the wounded self, and to take loving action for ourselves, others, animals, and the planet. That's what Inner Bonding is about.

Being aware of our intention is vital for being able to love ourselves. In Inner Bonding, there are only two intentions to choose from: to learn about loving ourselves and others, or to protect against pain with various forms of controlling and self-abandoning behavior.

Our wounded self is tricky: it can act like the loving adult, even mask itself as our higher guidance. This happens all the time with people: Their wounded self sounds loud and authoritarian and is sure it knows what it's talking about. But it's really just a child with a big megaphone and a loud voice. In reality, it knows nothing and has no access to truth.

By contrast, our intuition, inner knowing, and higher guidance are quieter. It takes mindfulness and presence to tune into our truth, to tune into whether or not we're truly being a loving adult. By learning to stay present with your feelings and intuition—your inner guidance system, and with your higher guidance—you can learn to move yourself more and more toward peace and joy

Different Parts with Different Needs

JL: Thank you so much for this opportunity to work with you. I obsess 24/7 because I have different parts that have different needs. I'm sixty-eight. I've been married forty-five years. I have no children, and my whole family and my best friend have died. My husband is my last attachment figure. We've both been self-employed, so neither of us has pensions.

I have been thinking about leaving this marriage but am afraid. Even with still working and Social Security, if I leave my husband, I will not have money at some point, according to financial projections. I have some friends, but they have very full lives and can't be there for me.

That's where the fear comes in of being completely alone. One part of me is terrified. Another part is truly attached to him. There's good and bad in this relationship. He has become addicted to pot and is a basket case. It's destroyed my opinion of him and our marriage. But I still love him on some level.

I'm very loving, and I have a very open heart, yet several times a week, I'm so upset by him: poor judgment, mood swings, one minute kind, one minute sneering at me contemptuously, which I cannot *not* react to. So there's the part that's attached and the part that's angry.

Dr. Margaret: That's a false belief: that you cannot *not* react to it.

JL: Okay. I look deeper and my mother was very shaming and critical of me. She was sweet and kind, but filled with shame and projecting it on me all the time, and pretty harshly. She would tell me how embarrassed she was by me. Other people's opinions were all that mattered to her. After she took me to her friends to socialize, when we would get back home, I would get yelled at for things in her imagination, even when I was two or three.

When my husband is sneering at me, I feel like I did with my mother. And if I say, "We have to address something in the house," he's lazy and unavailable. It's hard to get him to work.

Dr. Margaret: Let me stop you here, because you're highly aware of what he's doing, right? You're aware that he's contemptuous, and he says awful things to you. He is lazy, and you could go on and on with what's wrong with him.

JL: Right? It's me. I react so intensely to the sneering.

Dr. Margaret: The problem is that he's in his wounded self and you're reacting from your wounded self.

JL: Totally.

Dr. Margaret: There are good reasons for you to stay in the marriage. Obviously, it's scary for you to leave on the financial level, but it also gives you an opportunity to focus on what would be loving to yourself in the face of whatever he does. You say, "We have to talk about something," and he's not available, so why say this to him? Figure out how to resolve it yourself. If he's being mean or contemptuous, you need to learn to lovingly disengage so that you're not hearing him. It sounds like you believe that you can't help but react. I'd like to do an Inner Bonding process with you. Is that okay?

JL: Sure.

Dr. Margaret: Take some deep breaths, and breathe into what you're feeling regarding him and what's happening on the inside right now.

JL: Tremendous distress.

Dr. Margaret: Breathe into the distress, get present with it, and make a decision that you want responsibility for it. Breathe into your heart in step two, open to learning, and invite the love and compassion and strength and wisdom and courage and truth of spirit into your heart, becoming a loving adult. Breathe that in, making sure you're curious, open, really wanting to know how you might be abandoning yourself and what would be loving to yourself.

Now go back into the distress and ask your little girl what you're telling her and how you're treating her that's causing this distress. Go inside and let the distress speak.

JL: It's a sense of complete powerlessness. No matter how many times I express this, it's hurtful. It just happens over and over.

Dr. Margaret: So you have not accepted that you are powerless over him, but you are not powerless over *you*. The first thing that needs to happen here is for you to accept that you are completely and totally powerless over him. Saying how it hurts you is your attempt to control him, and he's not going to be controlled by you. You have to accept that, so there's no point in telling him your feelings or talking about what he's doing wrong. It's just hurting you. But you're not powerless over yourself. You have 100 percent choice over what you do in the face of what he does.

I'd like you to go into step four. Go to your higher guidance and put yourself in nature. Imagine yourself at a picnic table with your higher guidance and ask, "Am I 100 percent powerless over myself?"

JL: It feels like it sometimes, because . . .

Dr. Margaret: No, that's what it *feels like*. I asked you to ask your higher guidance: "Am I powerless over not trying to talk to him, not telling him my feelings, walking away? Do I have the power to change my own behavior?"

JL: I do, yes.

Dr. Margaret: So it's a false belief that you're powerless over yourself. It's a false belief that there's nothing you can do differently about yourself. Your wounded self wants to think that the only thing you can do is get him to change.

JL: Can I say one thing here?

Dr. Margaret: Yes.

JL: When I search my heart, I've always been extremely spiritually oriented. I had an experience about fifteen years ago when, by the grace of my spiritual teacher and the grace of God, love poured from my heart, and there was just bliss. But since he became addicted to pot, it's been a nightmare. It's drained me, and I've lost so much of the bliss that was inside.

Dr. Margaret: I have to stop you, because you're seeing yourself as his victim. Because he's done what he's done, you are the victim. You can't be loving; you can't take care of yourself. You are powerless. The problem is that you're seeing yourself as a victim of him, that he's taken all this away from you. As long as you're operating from that, you're stuck.

JL: Thank you. And it's my anger that I feel is destroying me.

Dr. Margaret: Let's move on with Inner Bonding right now. I want you to ask your guidance, what would be loving to your little girl in the face of what he's doing?

JL: What I get is to go by myself, have my own space, and leave the marriage, because I've lost too much momentum.

Dr. Margaret: That would be leaving before dealing with yourself. I never suggest that people leave before they change their end of the system unless there is physical abuse or severe emotional abuse. I don't think that's your guidance right now, because your guidance would be telling you to focus on taking loving care of yourself, walking away, spending time with friends, doing things that are fun for you, being around other spiritual people who can connect, and not interacting much with him.

JL: Right. And I do that all the time.

Dr. Margaret: No. Wait, wait. You're not doing that all the time. I'm suggesting that you stop trying to explain your feelings to him or talk to him about what he's doing, Stop trying to control him.

JL: Okay.

Dr. Margaret: Accept whatever he's doing, and be open to what would be loving to do in the face of it other than leaving him. You might have to leave at some point, but you haven't done this inner work yet. You still see yourself as a victim of him. You believe that you don't have choice. You believe that you're powerless over yourself. That puts you in a victim state.

JL: I gained that insight just now when you asked if I am truly powerless to walk away, or am I truly powerless not to open my mouth and say, this hurts me? I hear you. I didn't get that. But I do have that power now.

Dr. Margaret: Yes, you do have that power. I suggest that whenever he's behaving in a way that doesn't feel good to you, just walk away and take care of yourself in some way.

JL: The problem is, it's pretty much every day, all day long.

Dr. Margaret: I understand that. So pretty much every day, all the time, you're going to have to focus on taking care of you instead of controlling him. I don't think you realize how much you're trying to control him.

JL: I realized that more last night. I'm just catching on. Last night I got angry, and I realized I'm trying to control him.

Dr. Margaret: That's right.

JL: It seems like it's just coming from my heart that it feels like I'm being kicked in the stomach constantly.

Dr. Margaret: I'm going to put something out to you. I don't know the relationship and I don't know him, but it's my experience that when somebody is doing what he's doing, which is zoning out with pot and being angry, this may be a result of a long-standing system between you. The fact that you're getting angry, the fact that you're telling him your feelings to get him to change, indicates that there may be a control-resist system going on.

This may have been going on much longer than you think, where you've been, not consciously, but perhaps unconsciously, trying to control him. He may have been in compliance in the past, but now he's gone into resistance. This means it's time for you to deal with your controlling behavior before you think about leaving, because you're going to take that with you. This is not a resolved issue for you.

JL: Thank you a ton. I will be working totally.

Dr. Margaret: Okay, good. I'm glad to hear that.

2

Speaking Up for Yourself

How do you speak up for yourself? This is a big topic in relationships, because many of us grew up in families where we weren't allowed to do that. I wasn't. I just had to listen and do what I was told. I wasn't allowed to say how I felt, what I wanted, or what I saw happening.

When I spoke up, my mother would say, "Don't be ridiculous." That was her favorite expression. So of course I learned not to speak up. It has taken me a lot of practice to be able to speak up and have the courage to find out that if I do speak up, maybe the other person will care, maybe they won't.

When you grow up in a family like this, you learn to get scared of speaking up. It's hard to do when the person you're speaking up to doesn't care. That's what I experienced as I was growing up.

Having grown up in that situation, you carry that fear into relationships later. You think, "If I speak up, if I say how I feel or what I want, the other person is going to get angry or put me down."

Earlier in my life, when I spoke up, it was from fear. When you speak up from fear, you're actually speaking from your wounded self. Whenever we do that, our intention is to control. We cannot hide the energy of our intention.

As I've said, in Inner Bonding, there are two intentions: (1) the intention to control, protect, avoid pain, be safe, and (2) the intention to be loving to ourselves and share our love with others.

I was trying to speak up earlier in my life, but I was doing it from my wounded self. So of course when I spoke up to my ex-husband, he felt controlled, and he did not respond well to that. He hated anybody trying to control him. He would give an uncaring response. This in turn would confirm my expectation that I couldn't speak up for myself. It took me quite a while to understand that really speaking up for myself means being a loving adult.

Being a loving adult doesn't mean either putting your lower left brain in charge or putting your lower right brain in charge and acting like a little child. Being an adult means operating from your higher brain, and that energy is completely different. When you operate from your higher brain, people don't feel controlled or blamed or made wrong. They don't feel any of the reactions that they feel when you're speaking from a fear-based intention to control.

Speaking up for yourself means coming from love for yourself rather than trying to control. Very often when people speak up for themselves, they're handing responsibility for their feelings over to the other person: "I'm speaking up for myself; I'm telling you my feelings." That's not actually speaking up for yourself; that's making the other person responsible. "You hurt my feelings when you said such and such." That's a blame; that's an attack.

We all need to speak up for ourselves; otherwise, we're abandoning ourselves. But it's important to make sure that your intention is to love yourself and learn. You're saying what you need to say, but you're open to learning about how the other person feels or why they might have done what may have been hurtful to you. For example, you say, "You hurt my feelings when you said such and such, and there must be a good reason you said that. Can we talk about it?" You're stating your feelings, not as a blame, but with an intent to learn.

Getting present in your heart, connecting with your higher guidance, and being loving to yourself and the other is vital in a relationship, whether it's with a partner, friend, parent, child, coworker, employee, or boss.

You need to be aware of your intention but also realize that you cannot hide it. We think we can, and we think we can act as if we're open, but controlling the energy of the wounded self—if that's where we are—is communicated.

It's subtle, but I've seen it over and over in my own life: Whenever I speak up for myself as a loving adult, I have a good interaction, but if I'm speaking up out of fear and an intent to control, I don't.

Speaking Up to Professionals

Let's apply what we've learned about speaking up to dealing with professionals: doctors, dentists, attorneys, therapists, even building contractors. Don't give your authority away to anyone, no matter how much education or expertise they have, because nobody on the planet knows more about what's right for you than your own higher guidance, however you tap into that.

People often end up in situations that are not good for them because they don't trust themselves. They trust the authority, the professional. They're afraid to speak up because of how that authority or how that professional might react. I understand that, because many physicians, for example, see themselves as gods. They're supposed to know everything. If you question them in any way, they'll get upset. That does happen, so you have to be willing to lose the professional rather than lose yourself.

I take Armour thyroid medication. Years ago, when we had moved to Durango, Colorado, I needed a new doctor to prescribe it. I went to a doctor who didn't believe in Armour thyroid, which is made from animal glands (usually from pigs). He wanted to prescribe a synthetic thyroid. I had tried these, and they don't work on my body because it is so sensitive.

I asked him, "Would you prescribe Armour thyroid?" He said no. "But my body doesn't react well to the others," I said.

"Well, then," he said, "you'll have to find another doctor." Which I did. I had to find another doctor because he wouldn't do it. But I knew that my body would not tolerate another form of thyroid medication.

The doctor was mad at me, as if I didn't know my own body; I didn't know what's right for me. He knew better. He was the doctor, and he was playing god with me.

I don't want a doctor like that. I want somebody who works with me, not someone who wants authority over me. It's a matter of trusting yourself and of being willing to lose that person or have them be angry at you.

When you take the chance of speaking up for yourself, you're going to find out who this professional is. You'll find out whether they think they know everything and want control over you—so you'd better do as they say—or whether they're in partnership with you and will listen to you and honor your inner knowing.

The first time I went to my current doctor, I was really surprised. She said, "I think it would be helpful to you to do this. What does your intuition say?" She actually asked about my intuition! That says a lot about somebody, who they are, and whether they're in partnership with you.

It takes courage. Sometimes people are in difficult situations, like dealing with a surgeon. More than almost any other profession, surgeons tend to think of themselves as gods, holding life and death in their hands. It's hard if you have cancer and you need surgery and the physician is telling you one thing while your intuition is telling you something else. It takes courage to speak up and say, "No, that doesn't feel right for me. I need you to work with me, not try to control me." Again, you have to be willing to lose that professional.

Or say you're trying to get a divorce, and you're looking for an attorney. It's important to find a professional who will support you and work with you rather than someone who would try to control you and tell you what to do. I had one client who was going through a divorce. She had to interview fifteen attorneys before she could find one that felt right to her, who wasn't trying to control her or act as if he or she knew everything.

With Inner Bonding, you become your own authority. You become your own guru. It's not that you know everything. After all, you're going to a professional—a physician, an attorney—because they know more than you do. But that doesn't mean they have the right to control you. That doesn't mean that your guidance isn't here, guiding you in your highest good. It doesn't mean that you can't trust your feelings just because that person has had more education in a particular area than you.

Some technical people are highly left-brained and will discount what you know from your right brain—your creativity, your inner knowing, your connection to guidance. I feel fortunate in working with my webmaster and marketer, whom I found three years ago and who works in partnership with me. I'm happy with this relationship. We work well together because I respect his knowledge, and he respects mine. That's what we want in a relationship with professionals of any kind.

This is true with therapists as well. If a therapist thinks they know what's right for you and tries to impose that on you, that's not somebody you want to be working with. You want to work with somebody who helps you learn to trust yourself, who helps you learn to tap into your own knowing about what's right and wrong for you. Because it's not the same for everybody. We're all different, so we want to be in partnership rather than be controlled.

When I work with somebody, my goal is not that they should see me as the person who knows what they should do, but that they eventually claim their equality with me. When that happens, I feel I've really helped that person. To me, that's the best kind of relationship: where people are together with a sense of equality because they each trust themselves.

A professional might and hopefully does have more information about their area of knowledge, but that doesn't mean you shouldn't trust what feels right or feels wrong for yourself. Stay tuned into what feels right or wrong for you. Speak up, and have the courage to lose that person rather than lose yourself. Losing yourself doesn't work on any level in any relationship. I've worked with many people who went to a doctor or an attorney or a therapist and gave their power away. They often ended up with outcomes that were not good.

Inner Bonding is a process of learning to trust yourself and your inner, higher knowing, and staying open to learning with people who have information that you want. That's valuable, but not when they want control over you.

A Forgotten Birthday

Michael: It was my birthday on Monday, and it was my girlfriend's birthday a few days before that. I sent her a bunch of stuff on her birthday when she woke up and spent a lot of effort to make her feel good on her birthday, But the night before my birthday, I had this feeling that she wouldn't remember.

That's what happened. The next day, she forgot that it was my birthday. It felt really bad. At first, I tried to tell myself, "You knew she wasn't going to remember, so don't feel bad. You shouldn't have expectations."

After a few hours, I remembered that I want to be present for my inner child and not have any judgments. So I allowed myself to feel, and it felt really bad. I let myself feel how bad it really was without trying to judge myself or push those feelings away.

It took a few hours. I hiked about ten miles, and I finally got to a place of loving myself. I just kept saying, "I'm here for you. I'm here for you. Whatever you feel is okay."

The thing that was the most hurtful was not that she forgot, but that her reaction after I told her was mostly defensive. At first, she apologized and said she was sorry, but then she started making light of it: "Oh, well, ha, now you have a chance to do Inner Bonding." It felt unloving and uncaring. Maybe I'm projecting that onto her, even though I feel like it is actually a hurtful thing. I'm not a big birthday person, but the fact that she's my girlfriend and best friend and totally forgot, just felt bad.

Dr. Margaret: That sounds very uncaring to me.

Michael: Yeah. Then she called and said, "I did Inner Bonding, and my higher guidance said I'm not bad and I don't need to feel bad or guilty. Anyway, everyone has to take responsibility for their own feelings."

That felt like a kick in the balls to me. Yeah, it's true: She doesn't have to beat herself up. And it's true that I have to take responsibility for my feelings, but at the same time, I wondered, where's the compassion or empathy for how I'm feeling? It just wasn't there. It felt terrible.

Dr. Margaret: It sounds like she was using Inner Bonding against you.

Michael: Yeah. "Deal with your own feelings. I'm not going to take any responsibility for what I've done." That's how it felt to me. It's heartbreaking, you know?

Fortunately, I took a hike in nature. I was hugging the trees, swimming in the ice-cold water, nourishing myself in the sun, and connecting with God. That felt loving to myself. But I still feel really bad about the lack of caring.

Dr. Margaret: This is not the first time I've heard you experience her lack of compassion. You either need to accept that that's where she is or, if you can't, then not be in the relationship, but there's nothing you can do to make her different than she is.

She forgot your birthday. She wasn't compassionate about it. She turned it around and used Inner Bonding against you. It was a lack of caring. Definitely a lack of you being important enough to her to care about that. Either you accept that that is where she is in her life, or don't be in the relationship, but you can't make her be different.

Michael: Yeah. Finally I realized that I'm handing my inner child to her and expecting her to take care of him. That sunk in more clearly. I really am handing my inner child to somebody who doesn't always care, and why would I?

Dr. Margaret: Those are two different issues. One is whether you're handing your child over, and the other is whether or not she cares. I mean, handing your child over is you not caring about you, but handing him to somebody who's not caring or compassionate is a double whammy for your little boy.

Michael: Yeah. And it feels like the first one is critical. I was really committing to be present for my little boy and not hand him over. But I have to work on that, because it's not easy for me.

Dr. Margaret: Right. That's your challenge: to not make a woman responsible for your little boy. The other challenge is to accept that she might not be a caring person with you.

Michael: Yeah, that's a challenge too, because I love her, and I want to accept her as she is, but sometimes it's really painful.

Dr. Margaret: Yes, it is. It's painful to be with somebody who lacks caring and compassion at times, but you have to accept that, if you're going to be with her.

Michael: Yeah.

Dr. Margaret: We don't know what would happen if you stopped giving your little boy away to her. That would be the first thing for you to work on: not abandoning your little boy to anybody. Then see if that changes the dynamic, because she might be in resistance to your handing your little boy to her.

Michael: Yeah, probably. Definitely. She is also doing Inner Bonding, but I know I can't expect anybody to change or be any different than they are, you know?

Dr. Margaret: Right. But the real issue is right now for you to stop expecting somebody else to be the loving mom to your little boy that he needs *you* to be, and then see what happens if you're really taking responsibility for your own feelings.

3

Gaining Emotional Freedom

Almost everybody grows up emotionally dependent, because most of us had parents who were emotionally dependent, and that's what they modeled. They didn't help us to understand how to take responsibility for our feelings. If we don't know how to do that, we depend on somebody else to take care of them for us. That's emotional dependency: We've made somebody else responsible for our sense of worth, our sense of safety, our joy, our happiness and well-being.

No one has ever come to me without emotional dependency. If they knew how to take responsibility for their feelings, they wouldn't have come to me in the first place.

It's not as if everybody who seeks out help is emotionally dependent and the rest of the people aren't; it's that most of the rest of the people don't even know if they're emotionally dependent.

Inner Bonding is about learning how to avoid being emotionally dependent. It's about learning to take responsibility for our feelings and well-being. Our wounded self believes that somebody else can do it better than we can; they can love us better than we can love ourselves; our emotional well-being is somebody else's job.

That would be great if there was somebody else who wanted to take on the job, but there isn't. We're not infants. Nobody is going to be with us 24/7, tuned into our feelings all the time, or know what we need better than we do.

Overcoming Resistance

This is an important issue. Just about everybody I work with has some resistance to being a loving adult: They want somebody else to love them in the way they weren't loved. They also believe that if they're in a relationship, it's the other person's job to do it for them. When the other person doesn't, they think they have the right to try and control them. Of course that creates a codependent relationship and fosters emotional dependency.

What is your resistance to being a loving adult? What is in the way for you? What are your false beliefs? Most people have many false beliefs. Some think, "I can't do it." That is true of the wounded self, who's five or ten years old emotionally, but it's not true of you as a loving adult, especially in connection with your guidance. We're all capable of doing it as adults in connection with our higher guidance.

Another false belief: "Why try? There is no higher guidance: You're all alone in this, and you're going to fail, so why even bother?" I run into this over and over again with my clients. It's behind the false beliefs that generate resistance to showing up as a loving adult.

Another major false belief is, "I don't know how, I can't do it." That's true. We don't know how; how would we? Most of us had parents who didn't know how. There was no role modeling.

With Inner Bonding, the good news is that you don't need to know how; you just need to practice connecting with your higher guidance, because that higher self—which is always here, which is never *not* here—does know how.

If you've done anything creative, whether it's music or art or writing, you know that when you get into the flow, creativity comes through you. It's a great feeling when that happens. It's the same thing here. The source of your creativity is your higher self. Just as creativity can come through you, so can truth. The information about what's loving to you in any given moment is always there for you. You say to your wounded self, "You can't do it. You're only five or ten or fifteen years old. But I'm an adult, and I can connect with my guidance."

With the help of our guidance, we can learn to be loving adults. We won't always do it right. Personally, I'm always confronted with new situations. That's life. A new situation will come up, and I don't know what to do. I don't know how to deal with it; I've never dealt with it; how would I know? But I work with my guidance, and I learn, because nobody else is going to do it. Actually, nobody can do it the way that I can, because I am the only one that's tuned into what feels right inside. That's my inner guidance. I am the only one who can access my own higher authority. I don't give away that power to anybody else.

It's a great joy to show up as a loving adult. If you've never done it, you don't know what joy and freedom it brings. It's the opposite of emotional dependency, the opposite of neediness. It's empowering. It's such a joy to tune into your own true highest good, what's truly loving to you, and to do it.

We have control over that. We don't have control over other people or situations, but we have total control over our own intention. We have total control over the actions we take, whether we tune into our guidance or not, and whether we do what our guidance tells us to do.

Sometimes it's hard, but it's easier than trying to get somebody else to do it for us. Many people spend much energy trying to control what they have no control over, which is other people and situations.

It's not that control is bad or wrong in itself. I like having control over my intention. I like being able to choose whether

I'm going to try to control other people or whether I'm going to open to loving myself.

Accepting what we can control and what we can't brings peace. A life of emotional dependency is not a safe way to live. You're depending on other people for your well-being. There's a huge difference between that and emotional freedom. Emotional freedom comes about when we learn to show up as powerful, loving spiritually connected adults. That's what Inner Bonding is all about.

Losing Weight

Female participant: I have issues about losing weight. I've identified some issues that may have contributed to this. In my family, I was judged harshly if I gained any weight at all. I used to be thinner, but I almost feel I was rebelling against my family: "If you're not going to love me, I'll just gain more weight," which was dumb.

I gained a lot of weight, too, when I was taking care of my mom. I was helping her, and I was in a stressful job. Another thing: my dad yelled a lot. I almost feel like I get a reward from punishing myself, because that's how I got attention growing up.

Also, my inner child doesn't like to be limited in what she can do. She wants freedom to do whatever she wants, including with food, especially because I got squashed growing up while caring for mentally ill parents.

Dr. Margaret: First of all, it's not your inner child who wants to eat anything she wants. That's your wounded self, not the inner child. I encourage you to shift your attention from weight to health. There's so much about weight in our society. When you focus on losing weight, it will likely create a resistance in your wounded self: "No, you can't tell me what to eat. I'm going to eat whatever I want." When you decide to go on a diet and eat well, the wounded self is going to pop up.

It will say, "No, you're not my boss. I don't have to do that. I'll eat whatever I want."

However, if you focus on health, it changes everything. There's much research on which foods create health and which foods create illness. You'd be surprised at how many wonderful, delicious foods you can eat and still lose weight if you're eating healthy food rather than junk.

This is closely related to loving yourself. If you see and cherish your soul essence, if you really value who you are in your soul, you want a healthy body for your soul to live in. Then it becomes easy to eat in a healthy way, because you want energy and you want health.

4

Relationship Systems

Every relationship has a system. Some systems are loving and caring, such as two people who are taking loving care of themselves, including taking responsibility for their own feelings, and they come together to learn, grow, and share love. When you've been practicing Inner Bonding and you're taking loving care of yourself, you attract people who also take loving care of themselves. You have a much better chance of creating loving relationships.

But let's talk about the more common relationship systems: the dysfunctional ones. We abandon ourselves; we don't bring love to ourselves, so we want to have control over getting love from the other person. We do this in numerous ways. We might get angry and blame, hoping to get the other person to give us what we want. We might withdraw, withhold love, and shut down in the hopes of punishing a person. We might give ourselves up and be overly giving, overly nice. We might go into complete resistance as a way to push people away when they're trying to control us. These forms of control create a dysfunctional system.

There are overtly controlling systems, in which each person gets angry and blames. There's a lot of juice in that system, because there's a lot of energy in it, but there is also a lot of pain because both people are trying to control with anger.

Then there's a system where one person uses anger to control and the other gives themselves up. The one who's angry thinks it's working for them because the other person is giving themselves up. But the person who's giving themselves up hopes that the other person is going to give them love and approval. That never happens, because they're only reinforcing the other person's anger as a form of control. Eventually the one who's giving themselves up ends up feeling shut down and resentful, and no longer sexually attracted to the angry person.

Another system: somebody is controlling covertly by being subtly critical and judgmental. The other person hates being controlled, so they withdraw into resistance. This is very common, and I see it often with my clients.

The wife says, "My husband is completely shut down to me. He won't share his feelings with me. He won't sit and talk to me."

The husband says, "Yeah, but she's always criticizing me. She's always upset with me about something. She always wants to talk about the problems, and it's always my fault. I'm supposed to change."

The woman might say, "I wouldn't be so upset if you were to be more present and connect to me."

Then he says, "I'd be more present and connect to you if you weren't so controlling and critical."

You see the system. They're both right, and they're both wrong. They're both right in that they're each doing that, but they're both wrong in making the other person responsible, because each is responsible for their own end of the system.

They didn't just start doing it in the relationship. We start our end of these dysfunctional systems long before we meet each other. We learn them as we're growing up. If you think about your parents or others who you lived with, think about the system they were in. You'll see that you probably identified with one or the other. And you may be creating the exact same system.

I can't tell you how often a client will tell me, "I married my mother," or "I married my father. They're exactly like my angry father. They're exactly like my withdrawn parent." We tend to repeat, because we're operating out of our end of the system. We draw in somebody who is like what we've seen when we were growing up, and we're going to create the same or similar system as what we saw.

It's easy to blame the other person. Of course, that doesn't get anywhere. And that's why it's so important before you actually leave a relationship that's not working—unless it's physically or deeply emotionally abusive—it's better to hang in there until you have dealt with your end of the system.

Sometimes, when you do your inner work, the other person is going to get worse. If you're a caretaker and you're not caretaking anymore, they might get angrier and more withdrawn, and then you might want to leave that relationship. But when one person does the work of learning to love themselves and coming to the partner to share love instead of trying to get them to change, often the whole system changes. It's amazing that one of us can have such a powerful effect on the system.

Healing the wounded self is all about developing the loving adult, surrendered to and being guided by spirit, and taking loving care of ourselves. I can't tell you how much time it's going to take; it depends on you and how much you practice. But over time, you'll find that the wounded self starts to let go because it understands that you, with your guidance, know how to keep yourself safe better than the wounded self does.

It was an amazing moment for me when I felt the wounded self say to my adult, "I don't have to be so vigilant. I don't have to try and control everything because you're doing a better job of keeping us safe." There was a sense of letting go. It doesn't mean that my wounded self was totally healed, but it started to take a back seat. Life gets much easier when your wounded self realizes that you as a loving adult, with your guidance, know how to keep yourself safe much better than your wounded self does.

The Fallen Gazebo

JL: I'm unsure if I want to leave my marriage. One part says yes, and one part says no.

Dr. Margaret: Let's do some work with that. Please take some deep breaths and focus inside your body. What do you feel when you think about your marriage? What is the feeling about your marriage?

JL: There are two things going on at the same time. One is, there's anxiety in my body and stressful feelings if that part is thinking about the marriage. Then this other part feels like my heart, my child, just loves this person. So both are going on. It is terrible cognitive dissonance.

Dr. Margaret: I'd like you to breathe into the anxiety and decide that you want to take responsibility for your feelings. Breathe into your heart and be open to learning. Visualize your higher guidance and invite its beautiful qualities—love, compassion, strength, wisdom, courage, and truth—into your heart. Breathing that in, making sure you're an open and curious loving adult right now.

Now go into the anxiety and ask your little girl what you are doing or not doing, what you are telling her, and how you're treating her that's making her feel anxious regarding your marriage.

JL: It flashes up pictures of the past. I'm flashing up memories, not even so distant, which make her not feel safe.

Dr. Margaret: I would like you to stay current, and I want you to ask her currently how you treat her, what you tell her, what you do or don't do, how you abandon her within the marriage. Ask her today, how do I abandon you within the marriage?

JL: Staying in the marriage is abandoning her.

Dr. Margaret: No, no, you're missing the point. The anxiety is not because you're staying in the marriage; the anxiety is because there's some way you're not taking care of yourself within the marriage. What is it that's happening in the marriage that would lead you to want to leave?

JL: Lack of feeling of safety. Not from direct physical threat, but poor judgment in the partner, aggression, things like that.

Dr. Margaret: So the issue is that you don't know how to make yourself feel safe around that. You're making your partner responsible for your safety. You're saying your lack of safety is his fault rather than because you have not learned how to take care of yourself.

JL: Okay.

Dr. Margaret: Now you're saying you love him very much, and that's important information, but I don't think you're loving yourself in the way you need to in order to make your inner child feel safe when he's in his wounded self.

JL: Right, because there's always something that comes up almost weekly, and very bad things in the past. When I ask my inner child, she says she doesn't feel this is a totally safe environment.

Dr. Margaret: But you see, there's something for you to learn about making her feel safe. You keep wanting to go external.

But what do you do within the marriage that makes her feel unsafe?

JL: I think I'm afraid to forget, so that she's not wide open and blindsided by things. Like there's a protective thing, where I feel you can't relax in this environment. It's not safe. It's like I would be abandoning her without this more wary or vigilant part.

Dr. Margaret: So your wounded self says, "I have to be wary and vigilant, or she'll get hurt." That's self-abandonment, because the wounded self has no way of keeping her safe.

Let's imagine being in nature with your higher guidance. I want you to ask your guidance, what do I need to do differently to make my inner child feel safe without trying to change him? What do I need to do differently to take care of me?

JL: I could be more in my body. I'm out of my body a lot. I have to work at being in it, like doing meditation practices. I live almost outside it.

Dr. Margaret: That would make your little girl feel very unsafe. Safety means you're staying inside listening to your feelings, like having an inner baby monitor on.

JL: Yes.

Dr. Margaret: And that's step one of Inner Bonding. That's a practice. It takes time to get into your body, but as long as you're out of your body or in your head, there's no loving adult. That makes your little girl feel very unsafe. What happens between your husband and you that's so threatening? What does he do?

JL: It can be anything. We had a little gazebo out in the backyard. I said, "This is not safe. It looks like it's going to collapse any minute." He said, "You're being ridiculous. It's fine." But the gazebo collapsed within two weeks after I said that. Had we been in there, we would have been hurt. He is a dominating person. He's not hearing me, and it's often catastrophic.

Dr. Margaret: So you tell him that it's unsafe and he says, "No, it's not." Then what? It doesn't sound like you say, "I'm going to fix it," or "I'm going to call somebody to fix it," or "I'm going to do something about it."

JL: If I were to do that, he would be angry.

Dr. Margaret: So you're trying to control his anger by not taking care of yourself?

JL: Yeah. I guess I doubted myself, because he said he had just rigged it up; he had double-checked it. He knew for a fact it was safe. But the wood was rotten.

Dr. Margaret: So you're not trusting yourself and doubting yourself. That is a form of self-abandonment.

JL: Right. But if I trust myself and stand up for myself, it's just fight, fight, fight.

Dr. Margaret: You are coming up with every reason not to take loving care of yourself. Now if you want to leave rather than learn to take loving care of yourself, that's fine.

JL: No, I really would love to do that, whether I go or stay.

Dr. Margaret: But I hear every form of resistance coming up. "He's going to get mad." "I don't trust myself." "I'm out of my body." You've got every wounded reason here to not take care of yourself.

I want to suggest that your journey is not to leave at this point, but to be willing to start listening to yourself, getting present in your body, learning to trust your inner and higher guidance, and then see what happens. You have to be willing for him to get angry and learn to deal with that.

JL: Can you give me an example of how you would talk to yourself if the person you're with discounts what you say?

Dr. Margaret: If somebody discounts me, I just say, "I know what's right for me. I'm receiving guidance," and I just go ahead and take action on it. I don't hand that authority over to somebody else.

But you're focused on the other person's response rather than on what is loving to you and in your highest good. I don't focus on how somebody else is going to respond: "If I do this, they'll do that," or "They'll have this response rather than that response." That's not my focus. I don't have control over their response.

What I have control over is my own intention. If my intention is to be loving to myself and support my own highest good, I know that my actions will also be loving to others. What's loving to me is loving to others. What's in my highest good is in the highest good of all. I'm going to take the action that's loving to me and let go of the outcome. If the outcome is something that's not loving, then I'm going to deal with what's loving to me in the face of that. But I'm not going to try and control the other person's response, because I can't.

5

Overcoming Resistance

Resistance is a common issue. You can resist all kinds of things: getting up in the morning, exercise, doing your work, doing what you need to do. One of the biggest resistances that people have is doing their inner work, such as practicing Inner Bonding and learning to be a loving adult.

There's a good reason for this resistance: our wounded self. This is the self that we developed to survive the huge challenges that most of us had as we were growing up. We created our wounded self for survival. This part wants to control and wants to avoid pain and responsibility; it wants to protect itself against getting hurt.

The wounded self does not want you to become a loving adult. If you do, it means that you're connected with your higher guidance and then the wounded self is no longer in charge. This is the biggest shift you can make in life: shifting from having your wounded self guide you to having your higher self guide you. It's the most major shift we can make.

Resistance comes from the wounded self. It does not want you to make that shift because it loses control, and the wounded self wants control more than anything.

Often when I start to work with somebody, they'll say, "This is going to take so much work" or "This is so hard." That is the wounded self trying to convince you that this is too hard; you can't do it; your past is in the way. The wounded self has all sorts of reasons for you not to practice Inner Bonding and resist becoming a loving adult.

Another issue is that many of us had controlling parents. My parents were controlling. I didn't choose resistance as my main way of surviving; I chose compliance. But it doesn't really matter what defensive strategy you chose. We have all made a choice of how to deal with being controlled. When your unconscious choice was to resist being controlled, you developed a resistant aspect of your wounded self as you were growing up.

As I've often said, our wounded self is generally patterned after our parents and caregivers. So if you find yourself resisting, you might want to look at the fact that one aspect of your wounded self has absorbed the controlling voice of your parents or whoever was trying to control you, while another aspect chose to resist.

Tune into that voice, because that voice is likely saying, "You've got to get up early." "You've got to go exercise." "You've got to eat well." "You've got to get this project done on time." "You've got to do this, you've got to do that." Then, because you developed a resistant aspect of your wounded self, that part then resists, saying, "You can't tell me what to do. I don't have to do what you say," and you may then procrastinate.

You likely learned to resist controlling parents in an area that they couldn't do anything about. Kids will dawdle, be late, not get dressed, not get to school on time, or they'll hold in their bowels. They'll overeat or eat junk or they won't eat. Kids learn many ways to resist a controlling parent. It frustrates the parent, of course, because the parent can't do anything about it.

In short, resistance often involves an inner power struggle between the controlling and the resistant parts of the wounded self. The way out of it is to develop your loving adult, because when you're operating from your loving adult, those wounded parts are not operating. The loving adult doesn't put any pressure on you. It doesn't tell you what you should or shouldn't be doing, so it doesn't create the resistance. Instead, the loving adult goes to your higher guidance and asks, "What is loving to me?" "What is in my highest good and the highest good of all?"

Resistance can occur on either an inner level or an outer level. If somebody—your partner, your boss—asks you to do something, it may trigger that resistant, wounded part of you. You resist doing it or resist doing it on time or doing it well.

That's not what the loving adult does. Let's say you're in a relationship, and your partner asks you to do something for them. The loving adult goes to your higher guidance and asks, "Is it loving to me to do this?" If it is, you'll say yes, and if it isn't, you'll say no. But you're not going to be reactive. You're not going to either comply or resist, because that's what the wounded self does. You're going to go to your guidance and ask what's in your highest good?

Whatever is in your highest good will be in the highest good of your partner as well, whether they like it or not at that moment. Let's say your partner says, "I know I'm supposed to do the dishes tonight, but I can't. Would you do them?"

You go to your guidance and ask, "Is doing this loving to me?" Your guidance might say, "Yes, you've got the time. Your partner is really busy. Go ahead and wash the dishes, even though it's their night to do it." But your higher guidance might say, "You've had an exhausting day. You don't have time either. It's not loving to you to give yourself up and wash the dishes, even though your partner's asking for it." In which case you would say, "You know, we're both wiped out. Let's just leave it for the morning."

In either case, your answer would not be coming from a wounded place. It would be coming from your loving adult connected to your guidance. It would be a loving response.

I encourage you to pay attention to that controlling aspect of your wounded self, especially if you are resistant to practicing Inner Bonding. As I said, the last thing your wounded self wants is for you to practice Inner Bonding. You'll find all sorts of reasons not to do it: "I don't have the time." "It's not going to work." "I don't know how to do it." "I've tried everything; why should this work?" The wounded self has a million reasons to keep you from learning to be a loving adult and listen to your higher self rather than your wounded self.

Be aware of that controlling voice. Be aware of the resistant aspect of your wounded self. Be aware that you have a choice to shift your intention and be open to learning. Ask your guidance throughout the day, "What is loving to me right now? What is in my highest good right now?"

That's how you overcome your resistance. You can't overcome the wounded self from the wounded self, so you cannot overcome resistance and procrastination from the wounded self. Being aware of your intention is the most important thing that you can become aware of, because everything follows from your intention. *All your thoughts, all your behavior, all your feelings follow from your intention.*

Step one of Inner Bonding lets us know our intention, because if we feel anything other than peace and fullness inside, our intention is to control, protect, and avoid. We are in our wounded self. Of course you're going to find yourself there a lot, because that's what you've been practicing your whole life. That's why step one of Inner Bonding is being aware of your feelings. Your feelings let you know immediately what your intention is so that you can change it. If you want to, you can go to step two and shift your intention.

The Pusher

Hillary: I've noticed that in my work I'm getting really tired. I realized I'm operating from fear: that's what's driving me to work too hard, and it's coming from my wounded self. I call that part of my wounded self the *pusher*. It's not the loving part of myself. It's the controlling part of myself that makes me work so hard.

    I need to deal with this, because I love my work, but I'm feeling exhausted. And I don't like the feeling of being controlled by fear. When I was younger, I got myself into financial trouble a couple of times. I think that's the root of the fear, because I know what it's like not to have money and I don't ever want to be in that place again. I overwork to compensate for that fear.

Dr. Margaret: Take a couple deep breaths into the fear. Get present with it, move toward it, embrace it, welcome it as information, and breathe into your heart and open yourself to learning. Imagine your higher guidance, however you imagine that. Invite that love and compassion and strength and wisdom and source of truth into your heart. Breathing that in, making sure you're open, curious, and you really want to know. Now ask that little girl inside what you're telling her from your wounded self that's scaring her.

Hillary: I'm telling her I have to take care of us. I have to take care of you, and I don't want to be without. And I really enjoy having more than enough. So I'm willing to work for it even if it makes me tired. That's what I'm saying.

Dr. Margaret: So it sounds like your wounded self is saying that the only way to have enough is to overwork.

Hillary: Correct.

Dr. Margaret: Right. Okay. So how old do you think that wounded self is that has that belief?

Hillary: Maybe four or five. I think it comes from my family of origin. Fear is like a virus. I took on that fear. It's not my fear, but I didn't realize until this week how I was living that out in my life.

Dr. Margaret: So there may be a young wounded self that started to operate when you didn't have enough money. There may be various wounded selves in there that are saying you have to overwork to be financially safe, right?

Hillary: Yeah.

Dr. Margaret: That's a form of control. If I overwork, I can have control over being financially safe, right?

Hillary: Yes.

Dr. Margaret: Now imagine yourself in nature, sitting at a picnic table with your higher guidance. I want you to ask your guidance, is it true that I manifest better by pushing myself, exhausting myself, and overworking? Or do I manifest better by just being guided by you and what's loving to me? Which manifests better in my life?

Hillary: Well, when I'm with my higher self, it's like I know I'm always taken care of. I know I'm always guided. I know that if I follow God and listen, I'm fine. The door is open; work comes. This morning I got a feeling of my guidance being like a soft cloud that I can lie in and I'll be okay. And that I'm cared for if I just listen and don't allow the wounded self to drive me.

Dr. Margaret: You're saying you love your work, which is great, but you're exhausted. But it doesn't seem like it's the work itself. It seems like it's the overwork that comes from your wounded self pushing you from a place of fear and wanting to control rather than staying in your heart and being guided by what is loving for yourself.

When I'm in an open flowing place, I'm energized by spirit. When we're in that open space, we co-create with spirit, and we're plugged into a higher source of energy. When you're working out of fear—which means that your wounded self is in charge—it's like operating with a flashlight that's running out of batteries and you get exhausted. When you're operating in connection with spirit, it's like being plugged into an infinite source of electricity and you have plenty of energy.

Hillary: I experience that when I go to work. I can be exhausted before I go to work. As soon as I start working, I'm full of life, I'm full of joy, I'm full of energy, because I have learned to trust the leadership of the spirit when I work. But because I went into my own business, I had a lot of fear around making ends meet, so I overworked. I'd make a thousand appointments a year. I did that for a number of years, and all of a sudden, I woke up this year and decided, "I can't do this anymore."

Dr. Margaret: The exhaustion means that you're following the lead of your wounded self. Unless we're sick or we haven't slept, exhaustion around work lets us know that we're not tapping into the infinite energy of spirit.

Hillary: For sure.

Dr. Margaret: The exhaustion is a signal that's letting you know that your wounded self is in charge.

Hillary: Thank you so much, because I really want to stay in spirit. I love being in spirit.

6

Fear and Courage

When we talk about fear, we can begin by pointing out that there are two different kinds of fear. There's the fear of real and present danger, and this fear important to pay attention to. This fear might be warning you of danger, and this is the fear that comes if you're being attacked and you need to react: You need to fight or run or play dead. It's a natural reaction to real and present danger. This fear moves the blood out of your organs and immune system and into your arms and legs for fight or flight. It makes you stronger so that you can take care of yourself.

The other kind of fear is a real problem for us. It's the fear that has an acronym—*false evidence appearing real*: FEAR. This fear comes from your wounded self telling you lies, focusing on the future, making things up, judging you, ignoring your feelings, and letting other people define your worth. This fear causes anxiety by predicting bad things happening, which the wounded self has absolutely no way of knowing.

This kind of fear is the most common kind because most of the time, we're not being attacked. Even though nothing really dangerous is happening in the moment, you could be feeling a lot of fear because of what your wounded self is telling you. The body reacts the same way as with real and present danger: It goes into fight or flight. It pulls the blood out of your organs, out of your immune system, and into your arms and legs, and you feel stressed. It's the stress response. It's not good for you on a long-term basis. That's why stress is a major cause of illness. It's pulling nutrients out of your immune system because your wounded self is making things up.

My friend Susan Jeffers, who's no longer with us, wrote a book entitled *Feel the Fear . . . and Do It Anyway*. It's a wonderful book. It's about having the courage to do what you're afraid of.

When I first started public speaking, my wounded self made up all kinds of things that would scare me: "I'm going to forget what I want to say," "I won't have anything to say," "I'll say it wrong," or "Nobody will like it." If I had listened to my wounded self, I wouldn't have had the career I've had. Courage means recognizing that your wounded self knows nothing, refusing to listen to it, and doing what you intend to anyway.

The more you practice Inner Bonding, the more you are able to let your guidance come through you. When I speak about a topic in the masterclass, I know what it will be beforehand, but I don't think about what I'm going to say ahead of time. If I did, it would come from my wounded self or my limited mind. But because I've had a lot of experience in giving the task over to my guidance, I totally trust my guidance to come through me and say what it feels is important to say. When you practice Inner Bonding, you start to trust that. You start to trust that your guidance really does know more than your wounded self. That gives you the courage to do the things you want to do.

Take a moment to think about what you really want to do but are not doing. Do you want to learn to paint or make pottery? Do you want to learn to ride a horse? Do you want to write a book? Do you want to change jobs? Do you want to go back to school? Maybe you want to speak up—to speak your truth in some situation. If you're not doing it or you're procrastinating, your wounded self is in charge. It's scaring you by telling you, "You're going to fail. You can't do it. You're not smart enough. Bad things will happen." The wounded self gives you these messages to stop you from doing what you really want to do, because it causes fear.

Unlike the first kind of fear, this second kind is not the fear of real and present danger, because nothing dangerous is happening. Moreover, you have no idea about the future. Say you want to change jobs and you have to get some training, but your wounded self says, "You'll never find a job in this area" or "You're not smart enough to do this." The wounded self will say this kind of thing to stop you, and it thinks it is keeping you safe by stopping you.

I was recently working with somebody whose wounded self was telling him he was not good enough, he had made a mistake, and so on. But none of it was true. It was just causing a lot of fear. When he went to his guidance, he was able to get the truth in ten seconds, and all the fear went away. He was able to access the loving action for himself—what to say to a person he was having a problem with.

Our guidance is always there. It's just that we're not. When your wounded self is in charge, your frequency is too low to access your guidance, your source of love and truth.

The wounded self wants to stay in charge. It wants control. It believes that if you go to your guidance, it's going to die; you won't need it anymore. But at a certain level, the wounded self is instinctual, so it's not going to die, even if you do Inner Bonding. It's going to be there, but it just won't be in charge.

The wounded self is the part that doesn't want you to be led by your higher guidance. It will use any situation to pull you back down so that it stays in control. That is what it wants. This is what it believes will keep you safe.

Because my wounded self likes to control, I do a lot of things to give her other jobs. I've taught her how to control in ways that are not destructive, such as teaching her positive affirmations that quiet her down. Then she's fine.

If you want to accomplish something, do the six steps of Inner Bonding and go to your guidance for the truth. Recognize that your wounded self *never* knows the truth. Its whole basis is the core shame that comes from telling yourself that you're not good enough (a message that almost all of us absorbed at some point in our lives). That's the core shame, and it's low frequency. It will keep you from connection with your guidance.

You'll have courage when you are open to learning with your guidance. When you're operating from truth, you'll have the courage to define your own self-worth so that what you want to do becomes an expression of who you are. When you're doing your Inner Bonding work and you're relying on your guidance to define who you are, you will find that you have the courage to do what you want to do. Even if you don't know what you're doing yet, you'll learn.

I've learned a lot about being on the computer, even though my wounded self would say, "You'll never learn to do that." I don't listen to that. I go to my guidance and say, "I want to learn to do this. Will you help me or help me find the people who will help me?"

That's where courage is. I really want to encourage you: If there's something you really want to do but you're scared, notice that your wounded self is scaring you, but your wounded self doesn't know anything. Do your Inner Bonding work, open to your guidance, and ask it to imbue you with the courage to do what would bring you joy—even to have the courage to learn about your wounded self.

In fact, many are scared about doing Inner Bonding because they're afraid they might find out that they're not good enough. Of course the wounded self is not good enough—but that's not you, not your true soul essence.

Don't let your wounded self guide you. Let your higher guidance guide you in what you want to express. When you put your guidance in charge, you'll be able to paint or draw or write or whatever you would truly like to do. That's where the courage is.

Self-Worth Issues

Claire: You spoke of the two types of fear, the fear of real and present danger, and the false evidence appearing real. And I feel like I live more somehow in the second one, but that false evidence is real. To be more clear, I am aware that for pretty much my whole adult life, I've had issues around my self-worth, which has expressed itself financially. I've been self-employed for many decades and have just kept things on an even keel because I had a false belief that there was no pay for a lot of work that I was doing. So I did it for free, and then I did enough work to pay for the free work.

I am aware of pain in my body. I have shoulder injuries through my work, which now I can't do, and I find myself falling deeper and deeper into debt. I do have a new job, although it pays significantly less than the work I used to do. But it's like every time I turn around, here's another unexpected bill for thousands of dollars.

I don't even know how to work with this Inner Bonding. I do know it has to do with false beliefs. I don't know how to keep working with the pain in my body, and I don't know how to turn the ship around.

Dr. Margaret: It is scary to be in debt or not have enough money, so I totally understand that it's not something you're making up, but it is something you want to do something about.

Claire: Yes.

Dr. Margaret: I want you to breathe into the fear, get present with it, and make a decision that you want responsibility for that.

Claire: I want responsibility for this fear.

Dr. Margaret: Breathe into your heart and open to learning. Invite the love and compassion and wisdom and strength of your higher guidance into your heart. I want you to ask that little girl what you're telling her that's scaring her. Go inside and let her tell you.

Claire: She doesn't believe that I can help her with this, because I've never been able to.

Dr. Margaret: So there's a wounded part of you that says, "I can't help you with this." I want you to feel what's happening right now, Claire. You're going down into your wounded self.

Claire: I call it *collapsing*.

Dr. Margaret: You're collapsing into your wounded self. That's the problem here. When you say, "She doesn't believe that I can help her," she's talking about your wounded self, because that's what she knows. It's true: The wounded self cannot help you, but you're not the wounded self. It's scary for your little girl to not have a loving, spiritually connected adult here.

In short, you're going into your wounded self and scaring your little girl. The problem with that is that it's keeping your frequency low, and we do not manifest from a low frequency. We manifest from a high frequency when we're co-creating with spirit. When we're connected with our guidance, we're guided to what to do to take care of ourselves.

But you can't get there when you collapse into your wounded self. There's no way to manifest. Although people do create through control, intimidation, using others, and a complete lack of integrity, that's not you.

Claire: I'm grateful you said that because I feel like that's part of my block: a false belief that that is the way, and I can't hook up to that.

Dr. Margaret: No, that's not the way, honey. Yes, there are people who do that, and I get a few of them as clients, and I'll tell you why they seek my help: because they're miserable. They've got millions, even billions, and they're miserable, because they have gotten wealthy through control and intimidation, which is totally against their soul. It's in bad faith with themselves. That's not you; you're not going to be able to do it that way, and it's a good thing that you don't want to.

Now I want you to breathe into your heart, open to learning, and imagine your higher guidance. Put yourself in a beautiful place in nature. I want you to imagine your little girl, your soul. I want you to ask your higher guidance to show you some of the beautiful aspects about your soul. Your guidance loves your soul. What does she love?

Claire: She loves how caring and compassionate and sensitive she is and her appreciation for the simplicities and the natural beauty in life. Also, seeing the good in people. And the deeper way in which she loves to nurture projects or people or facilitate the well-being of plants. You know, that deeper awareness.

Dr. Margaret: She gets joy from helping and supporting.

Claire: Yes.

Dr. Margaret: That's beautiful. That little girl deserves to be able to express and manifest, and she needs you to have one hand holding spirit, one hand holding her. She needs you to bring that love down to her and manifest from spirit. That happens not when you're putting your wounded self in charge, scaring you and lowering your frequency, but when your intention is to love your beautiful soul. Of course you want to create financial security for her. That's when you can open to your guidance.

I want you to imagine you're in a beautiful place in nature, sitting at a picnic table with your higher guidance, and ask her what step to take or how can you create more financial security. The answer might not come right away. That's fine. But this is the kind of question you want to be asking. Your guidance does know the answer. Inspiration can come through, and you can manifest, but it has to be in that higher frequency state. So ask your guidance, what do I do?

Claire: My guidance is grateful that you said picnic table. It feels perfect, because it feels joyful, it's outdoors, and it's about nourishment. The first thing that's coming through is for me to be more at peace with my sensitivity. I think that creates situations where I either hide myself or I'm afraid that others are going to judge me. So I harden up in ways that I'm not even aware of. It's a protection, I think. Perhaps my authentic self doesn't come through as much because of this concern about my sensitivity.

Dr. Margaret: This is important for you. Have you read Elaine Aron's books about high sensitivity?

Claire: Yes.

Dr. Margaret: So you know that it's a gift.

Claire: Yes.

Dr. Margaret: And it's a really important gift for what you came here to do.

Claire: Yes.

Dr. Margaret: But your wounded self is judging you for it. Chances are that when you were growing up, you were judged for your sensitivity.

Claire: Oh, I was. And I still am.

Dr. Margaret: If you were to really own it, there would not be so much judgment. I was also judged for my sensitivity, but I don't think people dare judge me now because I couldn't do what I do without it, and I value it so much. I do everything I can to nurture, develop, and expand it in as many ways as I can.

This is what your guidance is saying: You need to own your sensitivity. And you need to be enough of a loving adult so that if somebody judges you, you know how to take care of your little girl. You own it and value it so much that if somebody were to judge you, you would say, "They're threatened by my sensitivity. This is their issue, not mine."

That's what a loving adult would do to reassure your little girl. This isn't about you; this is about them either not owning their own sensitivity or being intimidated by somebody who's sensitive, but that's their issue, not yours. It seems to me that your guidance is saying to you that this sensitivity is a big part of your ability to manifest.

Claire: Yes.

Dr. Margaret: But you have to fully own it. You have to deeply value it. You have to stop being afraid of being judged, because if you hide it, you're going into a low frequency.

Claire: I am at a crossroads. I think that I'm aware that some long-term relationships, including some with family members, may be ones in which I can no longer be as invested, because this part of me is not only not valued, it's frowned upon. And I think that feeling hurt is a piece of what's holding me back, but I also understand that in a certain way I'm giving away my power.

Dr. Margaret: Yes, you are. And you need to make a couple of decisions here. One is that you're willing to lose them rather than lose *you*, because you're losing you by trying not to lose them.

Claire: Yeah.

Dr. Margaret: The second is, you're willing to be hurt, because it does hurt when people who profess to care about you really don't.

Claire: Yes.

Dr. Margaret: You've been hurt. You can handle the hurt.

We've all been hurt in our lives, and we've handled it, so it's not the end of the world. But you have to be willing to lose them in order to be all that you can be.

Claire: I'm coming to awareness that this involves my whole nuclear family, so there's grief connected to it. This is really not new news. It's more facing the fact that this sense of not feeling supported or safe in childhood continues now. It's just not there in any aspect of my family.

Dr. Margaret: But as you own this sensitivity, as you value it and refuse to hide it, you might be surprised: Some people might pull away and then might slowly come back and actually value these qualities, because people tend to treat us the way we treat ourselves. It's vital for you to own this sensitivity, to cherish it, and to develop it. Then see what happens with these people. Okay?

Claire: Yes. This has been fabulous. I'm always so grateful for these times with you.

7

Remaining Happy Among Unhappy People

In this chapter, I'm going to talk about how to remain happy when you're with somebody you care about who's not happy.

Many of us may have been taught that it's rude or unloving for us to remain happy when somebody we care about is not happy. But if you think about it, becoming unhappy doesn't help anybody. It doesn't help you, and it doesn't help the unhappy person. It's you going down into a lower frequency. Rather than pulling the unhappy person up into a higher frequency, you're going down into a lower frequency. You're joining them, possibly because you're afraid that they're going to be upset with you if you're happy while they're unhappy.

If the other person is upset with you for being happy when they're not, that may be an indication of some narcissism. They may be unhappy because their wounded self is in charge, and there's often a lot of narcissism in the wounded self, which I call the garden variety of narcissism. That narcissistic aspect will feel angry or upset if you're happy and they're not. Realize that if the other person is unhappy, they're coming from their wounded self. That's no reason to join them.

There's another big issue here. Many people are empathic, as I am: I pick up everybody's feelings. That's both a gift and a challenge. If you're an empathic person and you're with somebody you care about who's unhappy, you're probably going to feel their unhappiness. That could pull you down. You're feeling their pain, and you care about them. You don't want them to be in pain, and you're taking on some of it. You are taking responsibility for their feelings. Many of us have been trained to be caretakers and take responsibility for other people's feelings.

Once again, this is not your responsibility. You don't help the other person by taking responsibility for them. In fact, you do the opposite: You disable them or enable them in the negative sense, because now they don't have to do their own inner work to find out how they're treating themselves and what they're telling themselves to feel unhappy. If they're unhappy because of an external situation, such as a loss, you can be caring and compassionate and comforting with them without also being unhappy or taking responsibility for their feelings.

Taking responsibility for others' feelings is not helpful to anybody. It's not helpful to you; it's not helpful to them, but it is a challenge to overcome it when you've been trained to do it. If you grew up with a narcissistic parent, you were probably trained to take responsibility for their feelings in one way or another: "Don't make noise; don't make Daddy angry." "Mom's upset. Go and comfort her; go put your arms around her." Conditioning can cause our sense of responsibility to run deep.

Of course, when you love somebody, you don't want them to be unhappy, but realize that being unhappy yourself doesn't help them. Like any addictive behavior, it may feel good in the moment to caretake them, but that doesn't mean it's healing in any way.

If somebody you care about is down, you can be there for them. You can say, "I can see that you're unhappy. Would you like a hug? Would you like some help?" Usually if they're in their wounded self, they won't be available for help. But if the person is available and says, "I'd love some help," certainly you can be there for them. You can help them, but you can't do it for them.

Becoming unhappy with an unhappy person is in no way helpful to anybody. Do what you can do to maintain your good feelings and your high frequency while being there for them, bringing love into you, and sending it out to them without taking on their feelings.

For me, it's been a big challenge, because I'm like a sponge. It's always been easy for me to take on people's feelings. I took on my parents' feelings all the time. I became the parent to their wounded kids, as many of us did: Many of us were parentified. It's been a challenge for me to keep from taking on others' feelings. I've learned not to do it with people I work with, and that's great. But with people in my personal life, it's been harder. I have learned to bring their feelings into my heart with compassion. Then I immediately and consciously say, "I give this to you, God. It's not mine to deal with." I feel compassion, and then I shoot their feelings out of my body.

This is what I do when I work with people. If I didn't, I'd be completely wiped out at the end of the day from taking on everybody's feelings. Early in my career, I would take on my clients' feelings, and I'd be wiped out. I learned to hand others' pain to God much quicker with my clients than with people in my personal life whom I love. But now I do it for both. I don't reject or disengage from the other person. I take their feelings in with compassion and give them to God so I can truly be there for them with love.

It will be helpful to stay kind and caring if the other person is available for that. Sometimes they just need you to put your arms around them and say, "I'm here. You're not alone." That's different from taking on their feelings. That's different from being unhappy because they're unhappy.

I hope you practice that. I hope you realize that it doesn't help anybody for you to be pulled into their lower frequency. But it can help them to stay in your heart, in your love, and pull them into a higher frequency with your caring. As I said, sometimes it's just a hand on their shoulder, a hug, saying, "You're not alone. I'm here. I care about you. I love you." Often that's enough to help them move out of a wounded state.

Bereavement and Loneliness

Lisa: I am coming up on the first anniversary of the death of my mom in a couple of weeks. I'm feeling numb, and I feel a lot of internal pressure to move forward with my life. I've had to make some changes, but at the same time, I feel quite stuck. My dad died when I was sixteen. I also lost my sister about fifteen years ago, so I've had a lot of loss.

Dr. Margaret: Let's do some work with the numbness. Take some deep breaths inside, into the numbness; get present with the numbness inside. Where does it feel numb in your body?

Lisa: Oh, it's the heart.

Dr. Margaret: Breathe into that; get present. Make a decision that you want responsibility for it. Breathe into your heart, open to learning, and invite the love and compassion and strength and wisdom of your higher guidance into your heart.

Breathe back inside into the numbness, and ask from the place of your spiritually connected, loving adult—being open and curious—what you're doing, how you're treating yourself, what you're not doing, what you're telling yourself that's causing your inner child to numb out. You're treating yourself from your wounded self in some way that's creating numbness. See if you can tune into what that is.

Lisa: The first thing that came up was that I'm scolding myself.

Dr. Margaret: So there's a judgment going. See if you can tune in. What are you judging yourself for?

Lisa: That I've ended up quite alone in my life. And I'm not able to have a relationship with my siblings.

Dr. Margaret: So there's a judgment from your wounded self about being alone?

Lisa: Yes.

Dr. Margaret: How old is the wounded part of you that judges you for being alone?

Lisa: I think it's young.

Dr. Margaret: What do you think was happening when you learned to judge yourself for being alone?

Lisa: I have twin sisters that were born when I was three.

Dr. Margaret: So you felt very alone at that time, is that right?

Lisa: Yeah. I was the only child, and then they were born.

Dr. Margaret: What the wounded self does—with just about all of us—is, rather than feel the loneliness and the heartbreak of twin babies coming in and you being alone, is to take it on yourself. You judge yourself: "What's wrong with me? Am I not good enough?" That's what the wounded self does to keep from feeling heartbroken and helpless over the situation. Because if it's your fault that you're alone because there's something wrong with you, then maybe you can do something about it.

Lisa: Yeah.

Dr. Margaret: So that three-year-old learned to tell you that it's your fault, and it is still doing that. It's judging you; it's scolding you: "It's your fault. What's wrong with you that you're alone?"

Then your little girl inside, which is the feeling part of you, numbs out, because that's painful. Your wounded self is causing you a lot of pain with that judgment. That's where much of our pain comes from: judgment from our wounded self.

Lisa: Yeah.

Dr. Margaret: Now imagine yourself in a beautiful place in nature. You're sitting at a picnic table with your older, wiser self, and your little three-year-old girl is there. I want you to ask your higher self, is it her fault? Is there something wrong with her?

Lisa: No. That's the first thing she said: "Oh, honey, it's not your fault."

Dr. Margaret: That's right. It's not your fault. There's nothing wrong with you, is there, that you ended up alone? There's nothing wrong with you that all these people in your life died, and there's nothing wrong with you that you're alone right now.

The truth is, we live in a society that does not foster community and connection in the way that tribal societies did. Nobody ended up alone there, not because they were better than we are as human beings, but because society was set up that way. Society is set up right now in a way that makes this hard. Many people are alone, obviously, but the numbness comes from the judgment.

Now I'd like you to take some deep breaths again, and I want you to tune in and see if you can go below the numbness into the sadness of being alone, the sadness of losing these members of your family. Just breathe into that, sit with that little girl, and put your arms around her and say, "I know that you want to connect with people. You know you want to have connected relationships, but you're not alone. I'm here, and spirit's here. We're not alone." Internally, bring some comfort in. How does that feel inside?

Lisa: It feels a little better. I don't feel so alone.

Dr. Margaret: Now I'd like you to go back to being with your guidance and say, "I want to connect to people. I don't want to be alone socially. What can I do? What would be loving to me?" See if anything comes through.

Lisa: Well, I am doing some things. I'm reminded that I'm in a group to support and develop my intimacy with other people. I'm also with you. I just need to be patient.

Dr. Margaret: Ask your guidance if there are any other situations that would be helpful for you and where you would meet like-minded people. I don't know what your interests are, but people volunteer in places of their interests, whether it's about what's happening on the planet or with animals or children or whatever. They find a place to meet other people who are like-minded. Ask your guidance if there's something on that level that would be helpful to you.

Lisa: The first thing that came up was that I did explore a dance studio that has dance classes every two weeks. I've been too shy to do that, but I'm being encouraged to give myself a chance to try that.

Dr. Margaret: Go inside for one minute here. I want you to ask your little girl what you're telling her from her wounded self. Now some of us are naturally born shy. I was, but I've learned to be more outgoing. I want you to ask your little girl what you're telling her that's making her afraid to do that.

Lisa: Two things. One thing came first, which is that I might cry. And the other thing that came right after that was, I might have fun.

Dr. Margaret: It sounds like your wounded self might judge you for both of them.

Lisa: Yeah.

Dr. Margaret: What if you made it okay to cry and have fun? It sounds like your little girl would like to dance.

Lisa: Yeah. I need to let myself do that. Because I explored it and then I kind of chickened out.

Dr. Margaret: So how does that feel?

Lisa: Well, it feels like I need to try that.

Dr. Margaret: See how it feels if you try it.

Lisa: Thank you so much. I really do appreciate it.

Dr. Margaret: You're welcome.

You can see that in the dialogue, Lisa and I are going back and forth in the steps of Inner Bonding. We started out going inside and doing the six steps. Then we go back down into what you're feeling, and then we go back up to your guidance and go back down to beliefs. It's a flowing process. You don't want to skip steps, but you do want to keep going back and forth and let it flow.

8

Healing the Fear of Rejection

Many people believe they're good enough and develop false beliefs about this. Here are some of the most common beliefs:

- I'm not good enough.
- I'm not enough.
- Other people are better than I am.
- I don't look right.
- I make too many mistakes.
- I'm inadequate.
- I'm not worthy.
- I shouldn't be here.
- I'm not important.

When we're rejected, we establish many false beliefs in our wounded self. It's almost impossible for a child to keep from taking rejection personally, especially when it's from parents or other family.

One of my favorite books is *Mister God, This Is Anna*. It's a true story about a girl who was found at four years old by a man named Fynn (who wrote the book). She had run away from home. Anna was an enlightened little girl. It's the only time I've read about a child who knew that the rejection and abuse she suffered had nothing to do with her. She realized that her parents were crazy and she had to get away.

The rest of us likely didn't run away from home at age four. I certainly didn't, and I took it personally when I was rejected. Then we incorporate our parents' wounded selves into our own wounded self, and we continue to reject ourselves in the ways that we were rejected. We treat ourselves the ways that we were treated or the ways our parents or caregivers treated themselves.

Whenever you're putting your wounded self in charge, you're rejecting yourself. Whenever you tell yourself, "I'm not good enough" or "I'm inadequate," you're rejecting yourself. You're rejecting your true soul essence.

One of the most important aspects of Inner Bonding is to connect with your higher guidance and see who you are in your essence. Learn to see the spark of the divine that you are—that we all are. God didn't make any mistakes in creating you. You are a spark of love. God is love. We are created in the image of God, which is love. Your essence is love, and you have your own individual gifts and talents and your ways of being in the world.

Think about it as if you had an actual child who is just like you were as a child, and you feel blessed to have that child. That's how you need to feel about yourself. As long as you let your wounded self judge you, ignore your feelings, give your inner child to other people for approval, and numb out your feelings with various addictions, you are rejecting yourself; you're abandoning yourself. When we do that, we continue to take other people's rejection personally.

This leads to fear. If you're judging and rejecting yourself, you're going to fear others' judgment and rejection. There's no way around that: As long as you're doing that to yourself, there's no way to not fear it from others.

Everybody is a spark of the divine, everybody is extraordinary, everybody has gifts. When you really embrace who you are, you naturally stop taking other people's judgments and rejection personally. You realize that they're just projecting onto you how they feel about themselves. It has nothing to do with you. It's not about you, because if they were seeing and valuing themselves, they would see and value you in your soul essence.

Another thing about rejection: If somebody is rejecting you, most of the time they're not rejecting your essence. They might not see your essence; they might not be able to. They may be rejecting your wounded self.

Everybody has to accept the fact that their wounded self is neither lovable nor likable. Nobody's going to like your wounded self. In relationships, somebody who's been operating as their wounded self will say to their partner, "You just have to accept me as I am." No. Nobody's going to accept you in your wounded self. The wounded self is no fun to be with. It is incapable of love and is often mean, angry, controlling, rejecting, and resistant. But it's not who you are.

So if somebody is rejecting you, they are likely rejecting your wounded self, if that's where you're operating from. You need to accept that because the wounded self is not a lovable part of you.

It can also happen that if you're operating out of your soul essence and being all that you can be, you might be rejected by somebody who's operating out of their wounded self. They may be threatened by your personal power—by your success, your creativity, your brilliance, by who you are in the world.

Unfortunately, there are a lot of entitled people in the world who want to maintain their position of entitlement, and they're going to be threatened by you becoming all that you can be. They might reject you; they might judge you. That's when it's especially important to not take it personally, because that's about them; it's about their wounded selves being threatened by you being in your personal power.

Nevertheless, rejection, judgment, and unloving behavior will never feel good. Unloving behavior will always create some heartache. If you're operating as a loving adult, rejection is not going to hurt your feelings because you're not going to take it personally. If it hurts your feelings, it means you're taking it personally, but it could hurt your heart because that energy doesn't feel good.

In those cases, you want to be aware that there's some heartache here and move into compassion for yourself. Say to your little girl or boy, "Honey, I know that person's unloving behavior hurts your heart, but I'm right here." You acknowledge the behavior, you bring in compassion, and the heartache will move through you. It's important for your inner child to feel safe to know that you know how to manage rejection, that you know how to lovingly manage other people's unloving behavior.

I have come up with a number of things we can do if somebody is being angry, rejecting, or unloving. It depends upon the relationship. If it's your partner, you have to know whether that person responds to compassion or touch. For example, somebody may be angry and blaming. Sometimes if you put a hand on their shoulder or arm and say, "Honey, I'm right here. You're not alone," they will soften.

In any case, you don't want to respond to what they're saying. If somebody is judging you, they're in their wounded self. You can't argue or get into a dialogue about that because you can't get anywhere with the wounded self. It's a low frequency. You can't get into the content. If somebody's angry, blaming, or judgmental, you can't get into that frame of mind. If it's somebody you love and you know that they respond to affection, warmth, compassion, or touch, you can offer that. If you think the person will be open to learning, you can say, "You seem really upset. I'm here. I'm listening. Are you willing to tell me what's really going on?" They might soften and let you in on what's happening.

But maybe you're at a party, and a person is not a close friend or is not open to learning or to warmth or affection. Then you need to lovingly disengage. Your inner child needs to know

Healing the Fear of Rejection

that you're not going to stand there and argue with them. You're not going to get into your own wounded self. You're not going to defend; you're not going to explain. You're not going to try and get the other person out of their wounded self. You're just going to say, "This isn't feeling good," walk away, and then deal with the heartache.

It's not easy. It takes a lot of practice to keep from getting hooked into your own wounded self when somebody's blaming or attacking you, especially people who are important to you. If you can't get into a loving adult state, sometimes the only thing you can do is to lovingly disengage.

Lovingly disengaging is not withdrawing, punishing, or pulling away with anger. It is taking your inner child by the hand and getting him or her out of the range of hurtful behavior, just as if you had an actual child and somebody was being mean: You would want to take the child by the hand and get them away.

Next, you make sure you haven't taken it personally, that you're not judging yourself, that you're not thinking, "If only I did this or that, this person wouldn't be acting that way." This means you think you can control their behavior, which you can't.

You are also bringing in a lot of compassion for the heartache, because there's always going to be a hurt heart when people are mean. It's really important to differentiate between hurt heart and hurt feelings. Hurt feelings means you're taking it personally. A hurt heart is natural. We're going to feel that whenever people are being mean, unloving, rejecting, or judgmental; it's never going to feel good. But they're not going to take responsibility for hurting your heart. That's your responsibility.

If you're in a relationship with this person, maybe later you can come back, talk about it, and find out what was going on. You can say, "That was hurtful to me. It hurts my heart when you do that. Can we find another way to deal with these issues?"

Over time, that might happen. It's not going to happen all at once, because the wounded self has been addicted to controlling for many years. But if you're with somebody who's open to learning, all of these things can change.

The Personal Growth Celebrity

Jolene: I've been working as a volunteer for a big weeklong event that involves a well-known personal growth celebrity. I've been to previous events with this person as a participant and have run into them at each event one-on-one, and I was like a kid seeing Santa Claus. "Oh my God! Hi." And I'd gotten hugs at each one.

We volunteers have a huge number of rules we are to follow. One stated at the beginning is, "Do not talk to this celebrity. Do not approach them. Just do not."

Yesterday we had a very deep meditation. After the meditation, I went to eat. I needed to eat by myself, so I was heading to a corner. As I was walking, this person was right there at a celebrity's table and waved to me. So I said, "Oh my gosh, hi. I didn't even see you." I went over and shared some of my experience, and then I went to eat.

Another person at that table reported me to the person who's in charge of us volunteers. As soon as I went back to the position that I was supposed to man, she called me into a room by myself, with her assistant, and shut the door. I was reprimanded severely and harshly. It was not a heart-centered reminder. It felt threatening: "I could end your week. I could take your position away. It's up to you. I know who you are. Do you have anything to say for yourself?"

I didn't get mad. I just shut down. I just said, "I'm sorry. It was not my intention. May I give you a little context here?" I shared that context, but it didn't matter.

"Yes, I understand," I said. "If I do it, other volunteers might think they can do it. I get it. I'm not a crazy stalker."

When I meditated on the situation later, I felt better. I talked to myself. I talked to my child: "You made a mistake. It's okay. You're not bad. You didn't do anything wrong."

But it was a very intense position. I got heart palpitations later in the day, and I had to go to the ER for a few hours.

Dr. Margaret: It seems to me that you're judging yourself rather than experiencing being at an event where somebody who works there would treat you that way. How does it feel to you to be at a personal growth event with somebody like that?

Jolene: I realized if they were that harsh with me, they're harsh with themselves. That's them. I can't control how they treat me or perceive me. As I've learned from you, I can only go into myself and be with my inner child. But I guess I was struggling with the rules and our code of conduct. We were representing the face of this celebrity. We had to be nice and smiley to everyone. At the same time, of course, all kinds of interpersonal dynamics were going on.

Dr. Margaret: If I were giving an event and I found out that somebody treated anybody that way, they would not be working there anymore.

Jolene: But should I report this woman or not?

Dr. Margaret: You should do something to say how badly you were treated, regardless of the rules. I don't understand rules like that. That doesn't seem to me to be a loving way of handling an event. If it's a huge event with thousands of people, and many of them would overwhelm this person, I can understand that. But they would have to better explain why that would be a rule: The person needs some privacy and can't be pulled on too much. How many people were at this event?

Jolene: Around 1,500 people. Sometimes there's many more. I've been at events where people try to get a piece of this celebrity.

Dr. Margaret: I can understand that. But it would have to have been explained in a way like this: "This person has only so much energy. When people go up and try to connect with them, it robs them of energy. So we would appreciate it if you would not do that." But the way that she handled it with you—to me, that is just not acceptable.

Jolene: It was because I said, "I know I'm not supposed to approach you as a volunteer, but . . ."

Dr. Margaret: Yes, you didn't follow the rules. But that doesn't justify this other person's behavior toward you. You're explaining this other person's behavior by your behavior. You don't control anybody else. Just because you broke the rules doesn't mean that you deserve to be treated that way, and I hear you excusing it: "I did this. I shouldn't have done that."

I think that you had heart palpitations partly because you did not show up as an adult for your little girl, who never deserves to be treated that way. Nobody deserves to be treated that way. That's what you're not dealing with. See if you can go to your guidance and ask what would be loving to you regarding this situation.

Jolene: Really listening to my inner child—is *protecting* her the wrong word?

Dr. Margaret: No. The wounded self protects by trying to control others. The loving adult protects by going to guidance and finding out what's loving.

Jolene: That's where I guess I'm stuck.

Dr. Margaret: Let's go back to you in that room. This woman was obviously harsh and reprimanding. If you had been a loving adult at that moment, focused on taking care of your inner child, what would you have done differently?

Jolene: I wouldn't have cowered. I would have stood up and said, "I take complete responsibility that I was aware of these directions regarding approaching this person. It won't happen again."

Dr. Margaret: "It's not okay to treat me this way."

Jolene: "I don't appreciate you speaking to me in this tone."

Dr. Margaret: *Appreciate* is not a very good word to use here. "It's not okay to treat me this way."

There are a number of issues for you to deal with here. One of them is breaking the rules. The celebrity waves at you. Instead of just waving back and going on your way, which is what you were told to do, I think your wounded self took over. You were not going to give something to him. You wanted something from him, which is exactly what they didn't want to happen. You could have just waved back, and that would have been fine. You need to deal with why it was more important to you to break the rules in order to get something from him than to honor what you were told. That's an issue in itself.

Then there's the issue of not taking care of your little girl who was being treated with such disrespect. These are things for you to work with. Your growth is to work with those two issues, because in both cases your wounded self was in charge. Your wounded self was in charge when you went over to the celebrity knowing that that wasn't allowed, and your wounded self was also in charge when you were with that woman. That's the problem: You're not showing up as a loving adult. Are you willing to do work with yourself on that? Because we obviously don't have the time to do all that work right now (because the time of the masterclass is limited).

Jolene: Yes, I am. Thank you for always smiling every time you say "a loving adult." I love it. Thank you.

9

Welcoming Your Sensitivity

According to research by psychologist Elaine Aron, about 15 to 20 percent of the population are highly sensitive. There's a test on her website (www.hsperson.com/test/highly-sensitive-test) that will take you only about ten minutes. It will let you know whether or not you are a highly sensitive person. If you are, it means that your brain is different from the brains of others. It is more sensitive. You're going to be more reactive to things—situations are going to affect you more.

Those of you who are very sensitive probably had some problems with that as you were growing up. I certainly did because I could feel things that other people weren't feeling. I could sense things that other people weren't sensing. I knew about things that other people didn't know about. I reacted to events that other people didn't react to.

When you're a highly sensitive kid, you feel there's something wrong with you. You think, "How come the same situation is rolling off this person's back? How come they're not affected by it the way I am?" It's confusing, especially if your parents are not sensitive. My parents were the opposite of highly sensitive. They were completely clueless, so it was really confusing to me that I could feel their feelings, but they couldn't feel mine. I was always trying to be there for them, but they had no idea how to be there for me.

The same was true with my friends. Looking back, I realized I was the only highly sensitive person in my group of close friends. It wasn't until I read Elaine Aron's books *The Highly Sensitive Person* and *The Highly Sensitive Child* that I understood the impact her work had on me.

I encourage you to go online and take the highly sensitive person test on Elaine Aron's website. It has a number of questions; if you answer yes to more than fourteen, it suggests that you are highly sensitive. If you are, it's extremely important to recognize that this is a gift. It is not a liability, even though it may have been growing up with it as a kid, and even though it may be hard now. After all, if you are highly sensitive, you're still reacting to things in ways that are very different from the vast majority of the population. That does make life challenging, but high sensitivity is truly a gift.

I wouldn't be doing the work that I do right now if I weren't a highly sensitive person. I feel blessed with this gift. If you find that you are a highly sensitive person, I do hope that you will learn to welcome it. Learn about it. Don't think that there's something wrong with you because you are highly sensitive.

When I was growing up, those tags on the back of shirts drove me crazy, even though most people don't notice them. I couldn't stand them. I always cut them off, because they're so irritating on my skin. In fact, when I was very little, I used to put my shirt on inside out and backward so that I wouldn't have the tag there. My grandmother would get mad at me because I put my shirt on wrong. What was wrong with me that I put my shirt on wrong?

Being highly sensitive, you're reacting to something that other people are not reacting to. Then of course there's the tendency to think, "What's wrong with me that I'm reacting this way?" I would get hurt by things that other people wouldn't get hurt by or didn't even notice. This happens a lot in families where there's one kid who's highly sensitive and the others are not. I didn't have siblings, so I didn't have that comparison.

Many people who work with Inner Bonding are highly sensitive. My clients will often say, "When I talk to my siblings about what happened in the family, they don't remember it that way at all." That's because they were not highly sensitive. They were affected totally differently.

Very often if you're the only highly sensitive person in your family, you become the scapegoat. Highly sensitive people can be vulnerable because we're reactive. In addition, if you're highly sensitive, you're usually also very empathic. People who are not highly sensitive can use your empathy to make you responsible for them; then they blame you for not doing things the way they expect. That can set you up to be a scapegoat in your family.

I was certainly a scapegoat in my family, and I still am, although I don't deal with it the same way. My parents, being atheists and clueless, thought I was nuts for creating Inner Bonding, having a spiritual connection, and being guided by spirit. That's hard, especially when you're a child and you're tuning into things that others think don't exist.

I encourage you to find out more about highly sensitive people. Read Elaine Aron's books and take the test. If you find that you are highly sensitive, embrace that part of you. It will serve you well—creatively, in relationships, even in work—once you understand it and value it.

In indigenous societies, highly sensitive people were the medicine people, the shamans, and the healers; they were revered. People were grateful to have these people in their society, but we live in a left-brain society, so highly sensitive people have not been revered. That's sad. Although I think this might be changing a little bit, it's going to take time.

A Frustrated Extrovert

Christina: I have a question regarding my feelings when I feel isolated. I work a lot from a home office. When I'm at the company, I have a single office. I had a breakup this spring.

I'm an extrovert: The more people around me, the better I like it. But often it happens—especially at the weekends, when I have no plans or just a few plans, some sports, some yoga—that I feel isolated. Instead of being able to enjoy the time or nourish myself, I can feel my energy drop because of the shame and the feeling of not being good or worthy enough. Then I cannot do things that I enjoy just by myself, like reading a book. I collapse on the couch with TV and food and sometimes smoking. It's like a drop in emotional and physical energy.

Dr. Margaret: Let me interrupt you, Christina. First of all, when you're an extrovert, you need to accept that you regenerate around people and that it's not easy for you to regenerate alone. You think, "I'll just relax; I'll read a book." But that's not what your inner child needs. Then your wounded self takes over and judges you. That lowers your energy even more, and you collapse.

Christina: Right.

Dr. Margaret: It seems to me that you're not accepting that you are an extrovert and that you need to be around people. Spending all that time on a weekend alone isn't actually in your highest good, but your wounded self is coming in and judging you, saying you should be okay with it. I don't think you should be okay with it, because it's not what extroverts need.

Let's do a brief process here. I'd like you to breathe into your heart. I want you to visualize your higher guidance and put yourself in a beautiful place in nature. I'm skipping some steps here and going right to guidance. Be with your guidance. I want you to ask your guidance what you can do that would be nurturing for you so that you're not alone. Where can you put yourself, what can you reach out to so that you're not alone on weekends?

Christina: She says what I'm doing already is try to make plans, try to be with people and do activities that I enjoy, like winter swimming, going on trips, or meeting people. I do that. I try, but I want to do it with nourishing people, you know? And yeah, it's a step-by-step process. I have to build up a bigger number of friends or people I can do something with.

Dr. Margaret: Where do you live?

Christina: Frankfurt, in Germany.

Dr. Margaret: So, in Frankfurt, do they have Meetup, the website where you sign up to get together to do something with other people?

Christina: Well, there's Meet5. I met some people, but sometimes they're a little strange.

Dr. Margaret: Many of my clients have met a lot of people through doing activities that they enjoy. One way is to join volunteer organizations; often lovely people join volunteer organizations. Whatever it is that's on your heart that you would like to support, that's a very good way to create community—through volunteering on weekends.

Christina: Oh, okay.

Dr. Margaret: Then there are communities that get together to meditate, or spiritual communities. Maybe an environmentally oriented group, like the Sierra Club in this country. There are many ways.

Christina: I think the critical part is what you said—that I judge myself for being an extrovert and enjoy being around people.

Dr. Margaret: Yes.

Christina: And my wounded self tells me, "You have to enjoy being by yourself; you have to learn that."

Dr. Margaret: See, that's the problem. You're not accepting the way you regenerate. We have to accept how we naturally are. I am naturally introverted. I need my alone time. In order to regenerate, I need to *not* be around a lot of people a lot of the time. But I used to judge myself for that, because more people in our society are extroverted than introverted. Some might say there's something wrong with me that I don't want to get together or go to parties. But I know this is me, and I need to honor that. This is you, and you need to honor that instead of saying, "I should be okay just reading a book." That's not who you are.

Christina: No, I love to be with hundreds of people.

Dr. Margaret: That's who you are, so as an adult, you need to do all you can to put yourself in those situations. Go to conferences, take classes. There are many things you can do.

Christina: I'm doing that already. But it's good that I don't need to learn to be alone.

Dr. Margaret: No, we all do need to be alone when we have to be. It has to be okay. But you don't need to spend a weekend alone, ever. It's not in your DNA.

Christina: Thank you so much for this.

Dr. Margaret: You are welcome. It's so important for all of us to learn and honor who we are. I am a highly sensitive introvert. That means that I'm like about 15 percent of the population. Most people are not like me. And I have to honor that. I have to honor my level of sensitivity. I have to honor my introversion; otherwise, I don't do well. When I do honor it, I do great.

Christina: Thank you very much. That's very relieving. I'll go for it.

10

How to Avoid Being a Scapegoat

Scapegoating is a situation where other people project their own self-abandonment onto you and blame you for what's going on for them. This is a very old tradition. It comes from the Bible, when the children of Israel were wandering in the wilderness after the exodus from Egypt. The Israelites ritually laid their sins on a sacrificial goat and sent it off into the desert. The Mosaic Law decreed that the priest "shall lay both his hands upon the head of the live goat, and confess over him all the iniquities of the children of Israel, and all their transgressions in all their sins, putting them upon the head of the goat, and shall send him away by the hand of a fit man into the wilderness: And the goat shall bear upon him all their iniquities unto a land not inhabited: and he shall let go the goat in the wilderness" (Leviticus 16:21–22).

The word *scapegoating* comes from that old tradition, and it's been handed down over the years in many different ways. In terms of dysfunctional families, I've found that it's usually the most sensitive child who tends to be most affected by what's going on. They're often more compassionate and caring, and they'll frequently assume the role of caretaker. That child is likely to become the scapegoat—the one that people are going to blame and get angry at.

If you come from a family like that, realize that your wounded self might have absorbed the false belief that other people's feelings are your fault, that you're responsible for them. You're just not good enough, and you need to be taking more care of people. This tendency can follow you into your adult relationships, where you might be the most caring and sensitive person in your environment, and it becomes easy for other people to blame you and to dump their unhappiness onto you.

I know this intimately because I was the scapegoat in my family. I was an only child, and neither of my parents knew anything about taking responsibility for their own feelings. I was also very sensitive and learned to be a caretaker, believing that if they were unhappy, it was my fault.

That enables people to scapegoat you: believing that their unpleasant feelings are your fault and that there's something you can do about who they choose to be. This is a big issue to let go of. It's not easy, especially when we grow up being caretakers, to realize that we don't have control. We're not causing other people's unhappiness unless we're doing it on purpose, but usually that's not the case. If you're not purposely trying to hurt somebody but are being scapegoated, other people are projecting their self-abandonment onto you. If it continues, it's because you're taking it on. You're thinking it is your fault. You're thinking there is something you can do.

If you feel you're being scapegoated, look at how you might be taking on responsibility, believing that other people's behavior is your fault. The wounded self tries to maintain control by thinking, "If only I change, if only I do things differently, they won't act that way." In order to feel a sense of control over other people's behavior, you have to think that their unhappiness is your fault. But thinking it's your fault puts you right in line to be scapegoated, to be the one that people are dumping their unhappiness on, making you responsible for them.

I want to encourage you to let go of believing that you cause anybody else to be who they are. We do not cause other people to act as they do. Nobody can cause me to be angry or blaming or defensive. Nobody can cause me to choose to be controlling. Nobody can cause me to be in my wounded self (which I will be if my intention is to control).

It's easy to blame somebody. Let's say somebody's yelling at me and blaming me for something I didn't do. I still have a choice. I have a choice to be a loving adult, to say, "I'm not engaging in this. I'm not available for being blamed," and disengage from the interaction. I also have a choice to try and control them by explaining and defending. That puts you in the position of being scapegoated.

Nobody but you decide whether you're going to control or whether you're going to tune into learning about what's loving to you. Nobody decides that for you. No matter what they do, they do *not* decide that for you.

In order to avoid becoming a scapegoat, two things have to happen. First, you have to let go of responsibility for who other people choose to be and believing you can control them. Second, you need to accept responsibility for who you choose to be and your own intention.

Of course, this is one of the biggest challenges we all have: to be aware of our intention moment by moment. Yet this is the basis of Inner Bonding. If your intention is to control, protect, and avoid pain, you're in your wounded self. The wounded self wants to convince you that it's in charge and it can come in any time, but it can't. It comes in only when your intention is to control. We have free will, and the essence of free will is choosing our intention.

If you don't want to be a scapegoat in your family or any other situation, be conscious of letting go of responsibility for others' feelings. And be conscious of being responsible for your feelings, of truly choosing the intention to learn about loving yourself. That is basic to the whole Inner Bonding process. You're not going to be able to go through the process if you're truly not open to learning about your own false beliefs, and about your attempts at control, and about loving yourself.

The Family Scapegoat

Layla: I've got a family issue. I'm scapegoated by the family. I have my dad and my two siblings; they are twins. I'm the oldest one, eleven years older. The twins are treating me like my parents did. They continue the pattern. So I have a bit of an issue with them.

Dr. Margaret: Can you give an example of what they do that makes you feel scapegoated?

Layla: When my mom passed away some two or three years ago, my dad sold the house and wanted to get rid of all the belongings. He wanted us to come up and put our names on all the things that we wanted to have.

One sibling has a small place, so she didn't choose very much, just small pieces. But the other one has a big house, and she came up before me and put her name on almost everything. When I came, her name was on everything, and it was shocking that she was doing that.

She called me some days after and said that it was wrong that she did that, because she and I should have just figured it out by ourselves, because our dad is not a big help here. I was calling him while it was going on and tried to talk to him about it. It was not possible, because he was blaming me for all the problems in the whole family and saying I was a witch, I was making all the problems in the family, and I was destroying his life.

I tried to ask what I was doing to destroy his life. He couldn't come up with an answer. How was I a witch? He couldn't come up with an answer. How was I causing all the trouble in the family? It was interesting for me to know that he couldn't tell me anything about that, because it's his own projection onto me.

Dr. Margaret: Obviously he was coming from his wounded self, or he wouldn't have said those things. That's a hard thing to accept that even though you might have been truly open to learning and curious, he wasn't. When we try to explore with somebody what's in their wounded self, we don't get anywhere because the wounded self makes everything up. It's not based on reality; it's based on projection.

Layla: Yeah.

Dr. Margaret: You're trying to talk to him rationally as a curious adult, but you can't get anywhere because he's operating out of his wounded self. That's something we all have to accept: We have no control over whether somebody's going to be open and honest and learn and grow with us, or whether they're going to project, accuse, blame, and stay in their wounded self. So right now, I want you to accept that you can't get anywhere with your father.

Layla: No, I had accepted that, and I'm not really talking with him. I see him when we are all together. I have not invited him to my home. I am only with him when there are other people around because he cannot behave himself. I know that.

But then there are the two siblings. A month ago, there was a funeral for an aunt who died. One sibling told me about it the day before the funeral, although she knew at least a week or ten days before. She waited until the last minute to tell me that to keep me from going to the funeral. She had done that two times before. All the family communication is going through those siblings, because I have been the scapegoat for so many years.

Dr. Margaret: And you can't go to the family directly?

Layla: I didn't know my aunt was dead. My sibling told me the day before instead of when she got the message, and she has done that before.

Dr. Margaret: Does that mean you couldn't go?

Layla: No, it was too late. I'm in Denmark, and the funeral was in Sweden.

Dr. Margaret: You can't do anything about them, so let's just do a little work with you, okay?

Layla: Yeah.

Dr. Margaret: I want you to take some deep breaths and tune into what you're feeling right now. What's the feeling?

Layla: I feel it's okay, but a part of me wants to reach out to the siblings.

Dr. Margaret: Wait. I just want you to go inside to what you're feeling inside—not what you want to do, but what you feel. What do you feel regarding the situation with the funeral or anything that happens with the siblings? What's the feeling?

Layla: It's kind of an empty feeling.

Dr. Margaret: Breathe into that empty feeling. Get present with the empty feeling. Can you make a decision that you want responsibility for that feeling?

Layla: Yeah.

Dr. Margaret: Okay. Now breathe into your heart and open to learning about what you are doing—not what they're doing, but what you are doing, how you're treating yourself, what you're telling yourself, what you're not doing, that's creating an empty feeling inside. Can you do that?

Layla: Yeah.

Dr. Margaret: Open to learning about that, and then visualize your higher guidance, whatever that is for you. Say to yourself, "I invite your love and your compassion and your strength and wisdom into my heart." Breathe that in. See if you can really own being in your heart as a loving adult, being curious, taking responsibility for the emptiness.

Layla: I feel that the empty space is filling up.

Dr. Margaret: But let's just move through the process, okay?

Layla: Yes.

Dr. Margaret: Just see if you can decide you want responsibility for that.

Layla: Yeah.

Dr. Margaret: Now breathe into that space that either was or still is empty. Your inner child is communicating with you through an empty feeling. Ask her, "How am I abandoning you that's making you feel empty? Am I judging you? Am I ignoring you? Am I staying up in my head and avoiding you? Am I using addictions to numb out? Am I making my siblings responsible for you? What am I doing? How am I abandoning you that's making you feel empty?"

Then go inside and let the answer come from the emptiness inside. What does that little girl want to say to you about how you're treating her?

Layla: It feels like I have given so much to those siblings and to the family, and I never really get anything returned.

Dr. Margaret: So your little girl is saying that you're making them more important than her? You're giving to them in the hopes of getting something back? You're taking care of them rather than taking loving care of her? Does that feel accurate to you?

Layla: I have done that, but I think I have stopped that, and I know I cannot change them.

Dr. Margaret: But that's not what your little girl is saying right now. She's saying, "I feel empty when you expect them to give back to me in the way that we've given to them. I feel abandoned when you do that." That's what creates emptiness.

Layla: Yeah.

Dr. Margaret: Instead of bringing all that love down into yourself and taking responsibility for your own inner child, you're sending it out to them in the hope they're going to care about you, and then they don't. Right?

Layla: Yeah.

Dr. Margaret: I want you to go a little deeper. How old do you think you were when you started to try and control them by giving to them in the hopes that they would give back to you?

Layla: Maybe thirteen.

Dr. Margaret: So realize that by the time you were thirteen, you learned to be a caretaker. You learned to try and control them by being there for them and giving to them in the hope that they were going to give back to you. When you're doing that, you're operating as your thirteen-year-old wounded self, expecting that if you give to them, they're going to give back to you.

Now let's imagine yourself in a beautiful place in nature, and imagine you as an older, wiser self, say 500 years older than you are. I want you to ask that older, wiser part of you, is it true that by doing all that I've done for them, I can have control over them loving me and caring about me?

Layla: Oh, no.

Dr. Margaret: Now ask your higher guidance, what would be loving to my little girl right now regarding my siblings?

Layla: It's to put a limit on them.

Dr. Margaret: On them or on you?

Layla: I'm putting a limit on how much I'm giving out to them, and I'm setting boundaries for them.

Dr. Margaret: You are still looking at it in terms of them—what you give to them or what you don't give to them. I'm asking you to ask for guidance about what you need to do for your inner child. What would be loving to your inner child? What does she need from you to feel loved by you, to feel important to you?

Layla: That I'm not abandoning her and not giving them my energy, but taking care of my energy and my own needs first, and then see if there's any left for them—if they behave okay or at least don't treat me badly. Because if they're treating me badly, I can't have a connection with them.

Dr. Margaret: That's right. But really the focus is on what you need to do for *you*. If you're focused on loving your little girl and going to your guidance for what's loving, you'll know what to do in response to them. But if you're trying to control them, you're going to end up being hurt and caretaking as a form of control. So your guidance is saying, focus on your little girl first, focus on your needs. Are you willing to do that?

Layla: Yes.

Dr. Margaret: Can you imagine doing that?

Layla: Yes. But it's still a bit difficult for me to have a connection with the siblings. I'm working on one sibling to have a connection. If she is showing me she has respect for me.

Dr. Margaret: I'm trying to help you have a connection with your own guidance, but you keep going outside that to have a connection with your sibling. I encourage you to work on the connection with yourself. Once you're much more connected to your own feelings, taking care of your own needs, staying connected to your own guidance, and creating your loving inner family, then it'll be apparent whether or not you can connect to either of them. But you're handing your little girl away, trying to connect to them without connecting to yourself first.

Layla: I can see that.

Dr. Margaret: So I hope you focus on your inner connection first.

Layla: Yes. Thank you very much.

11

Healing from the Mother Wound

Many people, both men and women, have a mother wound, a wound that we get when we didn't receive the nurturing or safety we needed. Many of us did not. Our parents may have done the best they could, but if they didn't know how to love themselves, they didn't know how to love us. They couldn't see who we were in our soul. As a result, they might have been controlling, neglectful, narcissistic, abusive, even sociopathic.

My mother was angry and narcissistic. Her touch felt horrible. It felt as if she was sucking the life out of me. I didn't get nurturing from her. I never felt loved by her. I was always trying to love her, which she could never take in. So there was a big mother wound.

I had a lot of therapy—many different kinds—before Inner Bonding. They didn't touch the wound, because none of these therapies helped me to learn to become the mother to myself that my little girl had always needed.

Ultimately, this is what heals the mother wound: when you practice Inner Bonding and you learn to be the loving, nurturing, present mother that we all needed until we were old enough to do it for ourselves. I didn't learn to do it, because there was no role modeling for it. None of the therapies taught me that I needed to be that ideal mother. Of course, when you don't see that anywhere, it's hard to know what it means, even though you can feel what you want.

That's why it's so important to develop a spiritual connection. You are certainly capable of doing this, provided you're really open to learning, eating cleanly, and keeping the frequency of your body fairly high. Then you can ask your guidance, "What does my inner child need from me right now as an ideal mother? Nurturing, bringing in love, listening to our feelings, seeing who we are, defining our worth, valuing our beautiful essence, discovering our passion, our purpose, our gifts." An ideal mother who saw and knew us would have nurtured us into being all we came here to be. The mother aspect of us is the nurturing aspect. (Of course, we need to be both mother and father. The father aspect is the aspect that will take action. That's step five of Inner Bonding.)

Years ago I read about indigenous tribes that didn't name their children until their gifts became apparent; then they named the children based on the gifts. I think that's beautiful, because they were looking at the child to see who they really were and nurturing that. If the child was particularly sensitive, they might have been nurturing that child to be a shaman or a medicine person. Nurtured in this way, the child will feel seen and supported in what brings them joy. Each of us has a blueprint inside of us for what we came here to do, what would bring us joy. For many of us, that was quashed and hidden because we weren't seen, but it's still there. Part of healing the mother wound is becoming the ideal mother who can see who you truly are.

You're not your wounded self. You're your beautiful soul essence. But you can only see this essence through the eyes of your higher guidance. That's why it's so important to be connected with your guidance: It allows you to see, nurture, and value who you are. When you do, you will stop trying to get love from others. You will stop doing many of the things that you're doing, like judging yourself to get yourself to do things right. This is highly unloving, coming from the false belief that if you do everything right and you're perfect, you can control other people, they'll love you, and you'll be okay.

When you show up as your own ideal mother and see who you are through the eyes of your guidance, you start to value and cherish your true essence. Something powerful happens when you really see and value who you are: You no longer want to give your inner child away to somebody else to be loved. You no longer reject yourself in the ways that you were rejected by your mother or father.

The mother wound is about being rejected for who you are. It's about being hurt or abused by the person who was supposed to love you, protect you, see you, support you, and nurture you. Now you need to learn to do this for yourself. When you stop rejecting yourself, and you start to truly value and cherish who you are inside, the mother wound is healed.

It's really amazing when this happens. I feel fortunate that I was able to do this before my own mother died. She was not an easy person to love because she was so angry, controlling, rejecting, and needy. But I did reach a place where I could see her essence. I could see her little girl, and I could be there and love her rather than always feeling the pain of her inability to love me.

When I reached the point of truly loving and seeing my little girl, I realized that my mother was incapable of doing this. I always thought she had the choice. Finally I realized that she was just too young a soul, and she was incapable of loving me, and that the mother wound would never be healed with her. It had to be healed with me. When I reached the place where I could be there for her, be the mother that she never had, and nurture her, I knew that I had healed the mother wound.

I also had help. It's helpful if you have someone in your life who can be a loving mother. I was fortunate. My best friend, cocreator of Inner Bonding, Dr. Erika Chopich, and I discovered mothering with each other. We discovered that we could hold each other like little babies, and be held and rocked and nurtured in the ways that neither of us got.

That was extremely healing. In fact, babies need holding for the first six months of their lives. Indigenous people know this. They hold them all the time. They hold the babies until the babies are ready to crawl off and start to be their own person.

When Erika and I started mothering each other, I wanted to be held for around six months, and then it was done. I didn't need it anymore. I was able to do it for myself.

If there's a motherly or a grandmotherly friend who can hold you in a way that you didn't get when you were young, this can be extremely healing for the mother wound. But it has to be somebody who has no agenda, who doesn't need anything back. The energy has to be clean to help heal the mother wound. There can't be any sexual energy whatsoever, which is why it's sometimes hard to have the healer be a man. If it's a loving man with no sexual energy, that can also help. It has to be a pure, spiritual, mothering, nurturing energy coming through.

The most important thing to know is that you can heal this mother wound by learning to love yourself. And you can support your healing by reaching out for mothering, if you have somebody who is capable of that. It's not always easy to find someone like that, but if you have such a person in your life, it can be particularly healing.

Dealing with an Alcoholic Mother

Lauren: After listening to your mother wound podcast episode recently, I was inspired to reach out to my mom. I hadn't been in contact with her for a long time due to her alcoholism. I sent her love, and I just wanted her to know that I have compassion and empathy for the choices that she's made—which I do—and I have a certain level of understanding. I just wanted to express that so she didn't feel like she was beating herself up for any pain that she inflicted on me.

I felt relief in that, and she responded by receiving it, and she said it meant a lot to her. That brought me a sense of peace. But there's still a part of me that feels a little bit resentful, because I feel I've kind of let her off the hook. It's conflicting with my intention to extend love and compassion.

I'm still suffering in many ways. It also ties in with my ex-partner, who's also popped back up recently, and with a horrible heartbreak last year, which brought me to your work. I'm forgiving, finding peace, and seeing the lessons as blessings in that situation. But a part of me is still scared to reenter it.

Dr. Margaret: Let's do some Inner Bonding. I'd like you to take some deep breaths into the resentment that you feel. Just breathe inside and get present with the resentment. Where do you feel it?

Lauren: In my heart.

Dr. Margaret: Breathe into that. Make a decision: You want responsibility for that. Can you do that?

Lauren: Yes.

Dr. Margaret: Now breathe into your heart, open to learning, and visualize your higher guidance, inviting love and compassion and strength and wisdom into your heart. Now ask your little girl if she's resenting you in any way right now. Go inside to that resentment. Let the resentment speak about any way she feels resentful toward you, any way that you might be treating yourself in the ways you were treated, or the ways that your mother treated herself.

Lauren: The first thing that came up for me was feeling resentful for not protecting her.

Dr. Margaret: Not protecting her when? Are you talking about as a child or as an adult?

Lauren: I'm thinking now as my adult self. My inner child may be feeling resentful in this present time for my being too slow to protect her and putting her in a vulnerable and dangerous position to be hurt again.

Dr. Margaret: So there are current situations where your little girl is resentful or angry with you because you're not showing up for her to take care of her in situations that could be harmful to her. Is that accurate?

Lauren: Yeah.

Dr. Margaret: How are you not showing up for her? What are you doing that makes her feel abandoned?

Lauren: Possibly bypassing how she really feels in the name of compassion and wanting the people I love to feel better and to not feel rejected.

Dr. Margaret: What I'm hearing is that you're an empathic and compassionate person, but you're sending it out before bringing it down inside first. You're not tuning into your little girl first before you're sending compassion out to others. Your little girl says you're doing that as a form of control so they won't reject you. Meanwhile, you're rejecting your inner child because you're not bringing that compassion to her, is that accurate?

Lauren: Yes.

Dr. Margaret: One red flag that I heard when you were talking about your mother is that you told her you felt empathy and compassion for her choices. You might want to take a look at that again, because I doubt that you feel compassion for her choices to be an alcoholic. You might feel compassion for her pain, but why would you feel compassion for her choice to drink?

Lauren: I guess I could understand, not necessarily why she chose alcohol, but why she's choosing that life to numb her pain or to make her pain less painful. That's what I have compassion for, and she's doing that in the best way she knows how.

Dr. Margaret: There's something for you to work with there, because there's a difference in having compassion for her pain that she doesn't know how to manage, and having compassion for how she chose to manage it. Also, your little girl is saying, "You're having compassion for other people, but you're not bringing it down inside to me." I think this is related. I think your little girl feels rejected by you.

You're a compassionate person, caring, empathic, but it has to start with you. Inner Bonding is bringing that empathy and compassion down inside, seeing what you feel, what you want, and going to your guidance about your highest good. It's also about sending love and compassion out to others, but not until you've really done the work on the inner level. It sounds like you're bypassing that. Is that accurate?

Lauren: In some moments, I feel like I am. In other moments, I'm not sure, because there was a period with my mom and with my ex-partner when I completely disconnected from them to protect my inner child, to protect my peace and my feelings. Now I'm at a point where I'm aware that it's my duty to protect my inner child first.

So I feel like I do have compassion for myself in that sense. But I'm getting stuck between having compassion and still protecting myself—if that makes sense—and not feeling anxious or resentful or scared to reenter these situations that cause me a lot of pain with these people that I love dearly.

Dr. Margaret: But it sounds to me like your inner child does not trust that you're going to show up as a loving adult for her in these situations. What you've done to take care of her is to completely disengage, rather than showing up as an adult in the moment of a situation. Is that accurate?

Lauren: Yeah.

Dr. Margaret: In order for our inner child to feel safe and feel loved in relationships, she has to know that we have done the work of learning to be a loving adult in the moment. Now this is a big challenge for most people, because we've had so little role modeling about what it looks like to be a loving adult in the moment of a situation.

I want to talk about one thing that ends up being a challenge for most people. In any interaction, there are two levels of communication. There's the content, like having an argument about time or money or whatever. Then there's the level of intention. One level is content; another level is intent. Many people, if somebody approaches them with an unloving intention, are tempted to deal with it on the level of what's being talked about: the content. This doesn't get anywhere, because then it's a discussion between two wounded selves.

Whereas if somebody's coming at you in an unloving way, like your ex-partner or your mother, and you were to respond to the intent, in other words saying, "I am not available to being treated this way in the moment," and disengaging in the moment, your little girl starts to feel safe. She knows you're going to take care of her. But for most people, it's a big challenge to remember to take care of yourself in the face of unloving behavior and refuse to engage with it. What's happening inside of you as I say that?

Lauren: It's giving me a lot of clarity. I feel a sense of ease that I don't have to be so scared to abandon myself or put myself in a dangerous position as long as I am able to respond to my inner child in the moment.

Dr. Margaret: It will make her feel safe to respond in the moment of what you're feeling, what your intuition is telling you, and what you're experiencing. But I do want to warn you that it's not easy. We don't just turn a switch and shift from dealing with content to dealing with intent. It takes a lot of practice, but your little girl will not feel safe if you continue to deal with the level of content when it's the wounded self who's in charge—the other person's, yours, or both.

Lauren: Thank you. That's really helpful. So would you say that I'm currently in a space where I should challenge my adult self by staying in this situation with my ex-partner and my mom?

Dr. Margaret: Here's the thing: If you pull back, there is no challenge. The way we learn this is within relationships. It's not going to come up if you're not in a relationship. So you might want to hang in there a little with your mom or your ex-partner, challenge yourself to respond differently, and see what happens.

But if it's physically abusive, I never suggest that people hang in there with any physical or intense emotional abuse, such as gaslighting. We just disengage from that. But in most interactions where people are in their wounded self, that's not happening. And it does give you an opportunity to practice. Whereas if you're just on your own, you're not being challenged on that level.

Lauren: Thank you so much.

12

How to Stop Feeling Like a Victim

How do we keep from feeling like a victim? Certainly many people have been victimized, perhaps as children by parents or teachers or others in authority, or by other kids. But there is a major difference between victimhood and simply being victimized.

I want to recommend a great book, because it's about this issue. It's called *The Choice: Embrace the Possible*, by Edith Eva Eger. Born in 1927, she's a psychologist who has traveled all over the world speaking. She is also a survivor—one of the last living survivors now—of Auschwitz. She was taken in at age sixteen. Both her parents were killed that day, but she and her sister did survive. She was rescued perhaps hours before she was going to die. She weighed seventy pounds, with a broken back, and had been brutalized for a year.

As its title indicates, the book is about choice. It's about Dr. Eger's journey in moving out of victimhood. It tells us a great deal about moving out of seeing oneself as a victim and utilizing any horrible victimization to learn and to grow and help others.

Dr. Eger helps us see how we have choices. Even when she was in Auschwitz, she made choices about how to take care of herself. What she thought and did saved her life. Later, she became good friends with Viktor Frankl, also a Holocaust survivor and author of one of my favorite books, *Man's Search for Meaning*. He was much older, and he became her mentor in the process of recovering from Auschwitz.

Dr. Eger could have gone through her life like some Holocaust survivors, blaming Hitler and the people who abused her. Many have, and many do. I've worked with clients who come to me miserable and ill because they've been blaming their parents, their partners, work, or God for their woes. They are putting themselves in a state of victimhood, where no learning is possible.

Dr. Eger had to do a lot of learning. She thought she was nothing. She thought that she was worthless. She had survivor's guilt. She had a great deal to learn about her false beliefs. In her book, she takes you on the amazing journey of how she did this. She ended up even being able to forgive Hitler, which amazed me. If she could forgive Hitler, we can forgive anybody. She didn't do it for him. She did it for herself, to free herself, to claim her freedom.

If you continue to see yourself as a victim, you have no freedom. You have given your power over to somebody else. You have given over responsibility for who you choose to be. As soon as you hand over responsibility and you're angry or blaming or withdrawn, you've put yourself in a victim state. There's no freedom in that. No matter what the situation, we always have the freedom to choose who we want to be at any given moment.

I remember reading about a woman whose adolescent son was shot by another adolescent. Instead of being an angry victim, she went to the jail and befriended the adolescent who shot her son, worked with him, eventually brought him into her home and adopted him. Talk about not being a victim! Talk about choosing who you want to be in the world!

We all have the option to choose who we want to be. I encourage you to read Viktor Frankl's *Man's Search for Meaning*.

He tells how staying connected to his inner knowing, moment by moment, saved his life in Auschwitz. He survived by not going into despair, staying connected to his inner guidance, listening to himself, and trusting himself. He was able to do that in Auschwitz and other concentration camps, and that's why he survived. That's how he developed his form of therapy, logotherapy, which became popular. I've learned many of the techniques that I use today from understanding his thinking. His book has been very important for me in understanding victimhood.

Victimhood is a low frequency. It's a difficult feeling when you let your wounded self convince you that you don't have a choice of how to think and feel and behave.

It's true that someone else might be victimizing you. Maybe you're stuck in a situation where you're being victimized. I hope not, because as an adult, you certainly have other choices. Even so, being victimized doesn't mean you need to see yourself as a victim or live in victimhood.

The way out is to become aware of your intention. If your intention is to have control over getting love, avoiding pain, and feeling safe through controlling behavior, you're going to feel victimized. You are on the wrong course, abandoning yourself in various ways; you're not treating yourself with love and respect. You're not taking responsibility for the fact that you are abandoning yourself, that you are not loving yourself or taking care of yourself, and disrespecting yourself. Often other people will treat you the way you treat yourself. Then you can say, "See? It's not my fault. I'm just a victim of this person," and keep yourself stuck in victimhood.

We always have the free will to change our intention to love ourselves, connect with a source of love, truth, comfort, and guidance, and learn what it means to take loving care of ourselves in any situation. I think of Nelson Mandela, who spent twenty-seven years in prison, was tortured, yet never saw himself as a victim. In all that time, he never lived in victimhood. He came out of prison to be president of South Africa and healed with the guard who tortured him.

I find these stories so inspiring. It's one reason I do a lot of reading. I love to be inspired by people who have made the choice to truly love themselves and found how deeply empowering that is for them. Imagine being in prison for twenty-seven years, being tortured, yet coming out in power. It's almost unimaginable that somebody had the strength to do that, but Mandela did.

That's so inspiring. Most of us are not spending twenty-seven years in prison. You may be feeling victimized in different situations, but hopefully you're inspired to recognize that you have a choice regarding your intention either to control or to love. It comes down to that, moment by moment. We have the choice to put the wounded self in charge to control, trying to get love, avoid pain, and feel safe. We also have the choice to develop our loving adult, connect with our higher guidance, and focus on what's loving to ourselves and others. That takes us out of victimhood and into a sense of personal power.

Feeling Unworthy of Honesty

Alyssa: I was in a place where I felt like I was stronger and I felt like I was moving out of victimhood. Then I recently found myself right back there, and it's been really hard to get out of it. My husband and I are definitely separating and getting a mediator, but now he's dragging his feet on it, and he hasn't stopped with the other woman either (laughs).

Dr. Margaret: I'm stopping you right now. You're disrespecting yourself right now by laughing at something that's painful. You just did that.

Alyssa: I'm crying, too, but you can't see it.

Dr. Margaret: Yes, but when you laugh at something that's painful, you're laughing at the feelings of your inner child, telling her that she doesn't count; she's not important. If you were in pain and somebody laughed at you, that would feel very disrespectful to you. But you're doing that to yourself. Laughing at your pain is a way to keep from embracing what you feel instead of taking responsibility for it. I just want to make you aware of that.

Let's do some Inner Bonding work. Take some deep breaths; use your breath to get inside and scan your body. What do you notice going on?

Alyssa: I'm feeling numbness in my head, like between my ears, and general pain overall, but just kind of a feeling of nowhere.

Dr. Margaret: I want you to breathe into that. That's your little girl communicating something to you with the numbness, emptiness, feeling of nowhere, feeling lost.

Alyssa: Like a block; she's blocking me from everything.

Dr. Margaret: Feeling blocked. Okay, so breathe into that and make a decision that you want responsibility for it. Realize it's your wounded self blocking you from whatever you need. Breathe into that block and make a decision that you want to take responsibility for what you're feeling. Breathe into your heart, open to learning, and invite the love and the compassion and the strength and the wisdom of spirit into your heart.

Now, ask your little girl what you're doing from your wounded self—how you're treating her, what you're telling her, what you're doing or not doing, that's making her feel this block, this numbness. Then go inside, and let the answer come from inside.

Alyssa: Just a feeling of unworthiness.

Dr. Margaret: I want you to breathe into the unworthiness and ask her what you're telling her from your wounded self that makes her feel unworthy.

Alyssa: I'm not worthy of honesty from others.

Dr. Margaret: How old is the wounded self that believes you're not worthy? How old do you think you were when you started to believe that?

Alyssa: As far as the honesty thing, I really don't think it was until I met my husband.

Dr. Margaret: It's not about honesty. It's about anybody's unloving behavior, whether it's dishonesty, whether it's anger, or whatever else it is. There's a wounded part of you, and the wounded self is always devoted to control. This is about control: Believing you are not worthy of honesty is a form of control. Because if you were worthy, then you'd have control over him being honest. This goes way back to you telling yourself that you're not worthy of being loved or treated with respect.

Alyssa: It probably goes back to when I was about five. My father told me he never wanted a girl.

Dr. Margaret: So you took that on as being unworthy.

Alyssa: Yeah.

Dr. Margaret: So you have a five-year-old in there that's in charge right now that wants to control, just like you did when you were five. Your five-year-old said, "I could have controlled my father's love if only I'd been worthy enough by being a boy." Which is of course a false belief: we don't control anybody's love.

I know a bit about your family. Your father wasn't loving to his sons either, so he just wasn't loving. It had nothing to do with you being a girl. But the wounded self wants to think, "Oh, if only I were different, I could have control." Is that right?

Alyssa: Yes, but I couldn't have been any different. I realize that. So why am I still feeling that way?

Dr. Margaret: It wasn't about you, and it still isn't. That's what you're not accepting. Your five-year-old is saying, "I'm not worthy of honesty." Do you understand that that's a form of control, of avoidance, to make it about you not being worthy—that if only you were worthy, then he would be honest?

Alyssa: Yes.

Dr. Margaret: But saying that to yourself makes your little girl feel abandoned, blocked, unloved by you. You need to see that, right now, control is more important to you than loving your little girl. Even lying to her is more important. You're upset at your husband for not being honest. But when you say you're not worthy, are you being honest?

Alyssa: Well, it's honesty in that I feel abandoned.

Dr. Margaret: Of course you feel abandoned, because you are abandoning yourself. Are you being honest when you tell your little girl that she's not worthy?

Alyssa: No.

Dr. Margaret: That's right. So instead of saying that you're not worthy of honesty, realize that you're not being honest. You're abandoning yourself and putting yourself in a victim state by telling yourself you're unworthy.

Alyssa: But I do think a lot of it is him abandoning the love of the family for someone else.

Dr. Margaret: I know you want to think it's external. That's what makes you a victim. You want to defend against the fact that this misery is how you're treating yourself right now. You're telling your little girl she's not worthy. That's self-abandonment. It comes from your intention to control, and that's what you're fighting against. You're fighting against knowing that what's happening is internal, not external. Just see if you can go inside and feel your resistance to taking responsibility for your feelings right now, wanting instead to be a victim of his choices. "He's abandoning the family. He's lying. Poor me. Look what he's doing."

Alyssa: Yeah.

Dr. Margaret: Now there's some good reason that you don't want responsibility for your own feelings for how you're treating yourself.

Alyssa: I don't know what that could be.

Dr. Margaret: Some good reason that you'd rather put a five-year-old in charge than your higher guidance. Let's see if you can shift right now and breathe into your heart.

Alyssa: Afraid that I'm not going to survive.

Dr. Margaret: That's the wounded self, but that's not based on reality. Let's breathe into your heart right now, visualize your higher guidance, and ask your guidance, "Is it true that it's my fault, that I'm not unworthy of honesty. Is that true?"

Alyssa: No.

Dr. Margaret: Is it true that I can't survive this?

Alyssa: No.

Dr. Margaret: Ask what would be loving right now to my little girl?

Alyssa: She needs me to be with her and know that I'm not going to abandon her.

Dr. Margaret: That's right. So imagine picking her up, holding her, and saying, "I'm here. You're not alone. Spirit's here. We're not alone. It's going to be okay."

Alyssa: I did that last night before I went to sleep. I had my little stuffed animal and I fell asleep with her in my arms.

Dr. Margaret: This is what you need to be doing. You need to reassure her. Refuse to let your wounded self tell her that she's not worthy, because that's self-abandoning. You need to be here as the adult that you are and let her know, "I'm going to be here, and it's going to be okay." What happens to that numbness when you do that?

Alyssa: It diminishes.

Dr. Margaret: I'm hoping you're going to practice this instead of indulging that wounded five-year-old.

Alyssa: I've been practicing lately, and it just came up on Sunday.

Dr. Margaret: It didn't just come up. It doesn't just come up. You shifted your intention. It's all about our intention, which we have control over; that is what we have control over. That is the essence of our free will: our intention.

Alyssa: Thank you.

13

Overcoming Rumination

I want to deal now with rumination. I am using this word in a very specific sense to describe a habit of the wounded self. The wounded self will go over something, over and over again, trying to figure it out and figure out how to do it right. It's obsessive thinking.

The wounded self uses rumination as a form of control. You're trying to control how you deal with a situation and the outcome. Sometimes you may ruminate about a partner or a friend. You go over and over what you're going to say as a way to control the other person's reactions. But that just creates stress.

Rumination may involve trying to control your own feelings, like a sense of loneliness and helplessness. Even if it creates stress, anything that's addictive covers over those feelings, and rumination is a form of addiction as well as a form of control and avoidance. Any addiction is an attempt to avoid deeper feelings, the deeper pain of loneliness, helplessness, heartbreak, and grief.

This is different from being in a loving adult state, where you're connected to your guidance and you have a problem that you want to solve. As an adult, you're not solving it on the level of your lower left brain (which is the location of the wounded self) by ruminating to control the outcome or avoid your feelings. Instead, you're in a creative state and you're open to learning, connected with your guidance. There's something that's not working for you, something you're not happy about, and you want to understand and resolve this problem.

This is very different from rumination, which comes from the intention to control. Creative problem-solving comes from an intention to learn about what is best for you, what's in your highest good. It's a higher frequency, and creative thoughts come in. You're not thinking the same thing over and over again, as you do with rumination.

Sometimes you wake up at night and get a thought that is important and that you want to remember. Sometimes the wounded self will think the thought over and over again to keep from forgetting it. This is a form of control. I suggest that you keep your phone or a piece of paper near your bed and write the thought down. Get it out of your head. Sometimes that will stop rumination. Even if it's a dialogue you want to have with somebody, write it down so that you don't have to think about it over and over.

That loop of thinking the same obsessive thought over and over is not a form of creativity; it is not going to solve the problem. And if you ruminate about a conversation thinking it's going to help you control the outcome or that person's response, that's a false belief. If you look back on times when you've tried to do that, you'll see that it has rarely worked well, because you're approaching it with an intention to control: "I'm going to think about it until I get it right, and then I'm going to do it right, and then I can control the outcome or control how the other person responds."

Whereas if you're in your loving adult and you have to have a difficult conversation with somebody, you ask your guidance, "What would be loving here? Do I need to open to learning about this? Or do I need to just talk to this person briefly, set a limit, and disengage? Or do I need to let it go with them, be loving with them, and take care of it myself?"

You can use the same approach in regard to any situation or problem. You open yourself to learning and give the topic to your guidance because that's where creativity comes from.

I had that experience recently. I had a work issue that needed to be resolved. I find that the time before I get out of bed is a creative time for me. I lay there, opened to my guidance, and presented the issue: "This is not working for me. I need some new ideas." I came up with a whole new model for what I want to do, and I got excited about it. As soon as I got out of bed, I wrote down the idea to go over with my webmaster.

I don't call that rumination. I call that creativity. It's such a different experience. I am focused on the issue, I am going over it, but I'm looking at it with my guidance to bring through new ideas. When I'm really open, those new ideas will flow through. I'm excited about what I came up with. That never happens if you ruminate. You don't feel excitement. You feel stress.

Recognize that rumination is an addiction. It's an intention to control—your wounded self believing that you can control an outcome or person or the feelings. You certainly can put a lid on your feelings, but you're causing painful wounded feelings by doing that. You may feel anxious, but the wounded self says, "It's better to feel anxious than to deal with the authentic feelings of loneliness or helplessness over others, or heartache or grief." That's not true for me. As an adult, I would much rather be with my deeper authentic feelings of life and handle them with compassion.

Again, it's all a matter of intention. If your intention is to control and avoid and protect, you're going to go down into your wounded self, and you might ruminate. If your intention is to learn about what's true and loving to yourself, you will go to a higher frequency. You will connect, flow, and be creative.

The Building Inspector

Kira: My heart is pounding because of the situation I'm in right now. I have a situation with my home. I got a notice from a building inspector that says that I'm not allowed to have my driveway gate or my hedges, so I'm feeling insecure and not safe.

I'm the one who actually instigated it. I have an Airbnb in my home, and my Airbnb got shut down because of this notice on my property. This happened years ago. At first the inspector just said to cut down the hedges in the front and he'd go away. That was sixteen years ago. But this new inspector says it all has to go. I have to take down all my hedges. They're eight feet tall. I also have to take down my driveway gate and the pillars out front.

Anyway, I'm so distraught over it. It's almost like when I was a kid, knowing that I did something wrong and I was going to get a spanking.

Dr. Margaret: So take some deep breaths. I want you to breathe into the upset, breathe into the feelings that you're feeling over this, and get present with them. Make a decision that you want responsibility for some of these feelings.

Obviously, there's an external situation that's causing you a lot of pain, but there's also something on the internal level. I want you to breathe in and say that you want responsibility for your part in this. Can you do that?

Kira: Yes.

Dr. Margaret: Now breathe into your heart and open to learning. Visualize your higher guidance, invite that strength and wisdom and love and compassion into your heart, and breathe that in. See if you can feel yourself in your heart as an adult, really open to learning about what you need to do to take care of yourself in this situation. Then go back in.

I heard you say that you have a wounded part of you who's telling you that you've done something wrong, and it's like you're a child getting a spanking. Obviously getting hit was unloving to you as a child, and it feels that way to you now. You have a wounded part of you saying you've done something wrong and you're going to get punished. How old is the part of you that's saying that?

Kira: Young—three or four, probably.

Dr. Margaret: So what's getting triggered is the three- or four-year-old wounded self who is scared, who is distraught, who is feeling like you did something wrong. Is that right?

Kira: Yes.

Dr. Margaret: See if you can go into that part of you and ask what you're trying to control or avoid or protect against by telling yourself that you've done something wrong.

Kira: I'm not sure. I get a little stuck on that.

Dr. Margaret: This is a painful situation, and there are deeper feelings here: the existential feelings of helplessness over this inspector ordering you around, telling you what you have to do. There's grief, there's heartbreak.

Kira: Yes.

Dr. Margaret: But when the four-year-old comes in and judges you for doing something wrong, that's a cover-up of your true feelings about the situation. That's not helping you find a way to deal with it. Because when you judge yourself as doing something wrong, you lower your frequency. That makes it hard to open to your guidance about what you need to do about this. You understand what I'm saying about that?

Kira: Yes. I'm ruminating and festering about it because I'm the one that welcomed them in. I didn't have to, I just wanted it to go away. So I contacted them and asked them what I should do. And that's when I got the brunt of it.

Dr. Margaret: So you're beating yourself up for having done that.

Kira: I didn't know what I didn't know until I knew it.

Dr. Margaret: That's right. You didn't know. So I want you to put yourself in a beautiful place in nature right now, and imagine being there with your higher guidance, your higher self. I want you to ask, "Have I done anything wrong?" I mean, other than not knowing not to reach out, but having the hedges or the gate. "Did I do anything wrong with that?"

Kira: No.

Dr. Margaret: I want you to see if you can own that you didn't do anything wrong. Now before we go on to what you can do, I want you to put your hands on your heart, take some deep breaths, and invite compassion in from your guidance. Let your little girl know: "Well, honey, of course you feel heartbroken and helpless, and you feel grief that we even started this. We wish we hadn't, but I'm right here with you and I love you, and you're not alone. Now I'm going to stop the wounded self from judging you and ruminating and beating you up for it, because that's not helping. I'm just going to bring love and compassion to you and move through the feelings of helplessness, grief, and heartbreak so that we can connect with our guidance."

Now I'd like you again to imagine being in nature. Be with your higher guidance and ask, "What would be loving to me? What would be in my highest good in this situation?"

Kira: To let it go.

Dr. Margaret: What does that mean, let go?

Kira: To let it go, like to stop dwelling on it.

Dr. Margaret: But is there anything you can do? Can you hire an attorney to get this changed?

Kira: I've already tried. I've called everybody. I've called attorneys; I've called builders. I even called my city council to see if they can help me, but no.

Dr. Margaret: Why not?

Kira: They say I'm breaking the law even though these things have been on my property for twenty-five years. All of a sudden, I'm breaking the law because somebody complained.

Dr. Margaret: Somebody complained?

Kira: Yep. Four years ago someone complained, and it just came up now in the system.

Dr. Margaret: So it's not necessarily you asking them to come out, it's that somebody complained?

Kira: Somebody complained four years ago, and I'm the one that wanted my Airbnb back up. So I said, "What do I need to do to comply?" That's when I got all the laws that I didn't know about. I didn't know I wasn't allowed to have a fence or hedges.

Dr. Margaret: So if you want your Airbnb, then you need to comply. Is that right?

Kira: Yep.

Dr. Margaret: Which would you rather do: comply or not have your Airbnb?

Kira: Right now, it's too late. I can't have either. I have to comply. And then I don't know if they're going to allow me to have the Airbnb. It's a big question mark. I don't have all the answers. I keep reaching out to find out what the steps are. Then I have to pay money. If I want to keep it, I have to take the hedge down to three and a half feet. It's eight feet, so you can see how much it would cost. Then I feel like I would be completely exposed. But they said that, even to keep it, I have to pay permit fees, because none of it's permitted. I'm just in shock. I've been here for so long, and it's mind-blowing.

Dr. Margaret: What would happen if you didn't do anything?

Kira: I would have to pay fines. They could fine me up to $500 or $600 a day for not complying. They're just not helpful at all. There's no wiggle room; there's no leeway. You either do what we say or else.

Dr. Margaret: It's obviously unfair. Here, near Denver, Colorado, we have a television station where you can bring unfair situations like this, and they will investigate and help. Do you have anything like that where you are?

Kira: Not exactly like that. I guess I could go to the media.

Dr. Margaret: You might want to look into seeing if you do have a television station like that, because here they help people a lot with these situations. They look into the unfairness, they interview the people involved, and they do all kinds of things to be helpful. You might want to look into that and see. If you don't have something like that, you might need to just comply and see where it goes.

I can assure you that if you were to stop ruminating and open to learning about what's loving to you, you might get some information that would be helpful to you. Are you willing to do that?

Kira: Yes, I am.

14

Previous Trauma and Personal Strength

The relationship between previous trauma and personal strength—and here I mean emotional rather than physical strength—is complex. On the one hand, when children have been abused and traumatized, they've often had to develop deep methods of resilience. In that sense, childhood trauma can lead to strength. On the other hand, trauma can be absorbed into the wounded self and undermine knowing who you are.

The difference depends upon intention. I've known people in the same family, all of whom were badly abused. Often one person will be open, go into therapy, do their healing work, and learn to define who they are. They heal their false beliefs and come into their personal power, while the other kids in the family remain feeling like victims. They never move into their personal power.

When someone has the intention to learn, they utilize their situation—including past traumas—to move into their personal power. The same is true with adult trauma from spouses, illness, or injuries. Physical illness can come from many different sources: It can be hereditary. It can come from not taking good care of yourself with what you eat. It can come from trauma. It can come from unhealed childhood abuse.

In any case, moving into your personal power is about your intention: refusing to see yourself as a victim of your spouse or your illness, but doing the work to take as much responsibility as possible. It is possible to take any challenge in life and utilize it as a learning opportunity. Utilize what happened with your spouse or your illness to move into deeper and deeper levels of personal responsibility.

Personal responsibility can take many forms. A house that was flooded and has had mold for decades can undermine stamina, cause fever, and leave you bedridden for a year. Although that is not something that you caused, it is a problem that you can research. Mold can be extremely toxic, but there are many ways of dealing with it. I have numerous clients who have become very ill from mold, but they do their research. There are practitioners that know how to take the mold out of your body. Even so, it is still going to be up to you to do the work of finding what you need to help you heal.

This is why Inner Bonding is so powerful for any form of trauma. It's about how you treat yourself in the face of it. Are you doing the work of developing the loving adult? Inner Bonding develops new neural pathways in the brain, so you have an inner resource that you didn't have before. Are you developing new neural pathways in your brain through Inner Bonding so that every day you're showing up more and more as a loving adult? All of us learned to develop our wounded self in the lower left brain. Few of us learned to develop the neural pathways in our higher brain for the loving adult, especially regarding emotional responsibility, because we didn't have the role modeling.

Healing from any kind of trauma is about being devoted to learning, taking loving care of yourself, and developing your spiritual connection so that you can determine what's in your highest good.

The information is there for us when we're open to it, but sometimes you don't get it immediately. On one occasion, I was out walking with my dog, and I was pondering a dilemma that I needed to resolve in the next few months. From my point of view, neither alternative was that great, but I needed to decide, so I had been asking my guidance repeatedly.

Finally it came through clearly: "It's not time yet. You can't know the answer yet." I had to accept that I needed to be closer to the time when I had to make the decision before I could really know my highest good in this situation. But I knew I would get that information. My guidance clearly said, "You're going to get more information in the next few months." To me, that was quite empowering.

There's a quote from an Indian philosopher that I like: "Pain is the hand of nature sculpturing men and women to their greatness." That is how we grow. Many people who come from comparatively easy backgrounds don't choose to learn and grow until something bad happens. It's sad that often we have to be motivated by pain, but it's true. Nobody likes pain, but it can move you toward your strength, personal power, and resilience—even toward the information you need.

Some may wonder how we know that Inner Bonding develops new neural pathways in the brain. I know from my own experience and the experience of thousands of people that I've worked with. I can't tell you that we've done MRIs to prove that this practice creates new neural pathways. But I can tell you from my experience from the anecdotal evidence of thousands of people I've worked with.

Many people say, "My brain has changed. I am different. I now have something to turn to that I didn't have before." The only way you're going to know for yourself is to practice Inner Bonding and see what happens with your own brain.

Redoing Past Trauma

Polly: I was an abused kid in every way: physically, sexually, verbally, you name it. I was doing this exercise in a book where you're supposed to write about how you're feeling from your innocent inner child. I was having a hard time because I realized I lay all this stuff on top of that innocent child—shame, or, I don't know what else, numbness. I don't seem to get fully present in the moment and be vulnerable.

I think a lot of it goes back to trying to protect myself from abuse. I'm not fully present in my feelings. I know that practicing and tuning into my feelings help, like breathing in my body. But I don't know if there are other things I could do to get to that innocent place before all the abuse.

Dr. Margaret: When you've had that much abuse, there may be more than one child in there. They don't feel safe in letting you in on what's going on until they trust that there's a really strong, loving adult who knows how to manage the feelings.

When I work with somebody who's had a lot of abuse—and I work with many people who have—I don't go directly into the feeling part because they're not strong enough yet to be dealing with that. I work primarily with developing a loving adult.

That's what I encourage you to do: Work with your higher guidance if you can, or get some facilitation in developing your loving adult. The six steps of Inner Bonding develop your loving adult as you increasingly open to your higher guidance instead of to your feelings. Start to take loving action today for your little girl. The more you learn to become a loving mom and dad for your little girl, the more your little girl will trust you.

The other thing that you can do to help your little girl to trust you is to redo situations. If you're willing to do that with me now, I can bring you through that. Can you tell me a specific incident of abuse?

Polly: One incident was when I was in high school. My mom read my diary, and she told me I was a bad kid. She said she wished she never had me, and then she left for years after that.

Dr. Margaret: So let's imagine that you are at your present age. Are you in connection with a higher source of guidance?

Polly: No.

Margaret: Please imagine an older, wiser part of you, like 500 years older than you are—very loving, powerful, and wise. Can you do that?

Polly: Yes

Dr. Margaret: Now imagine that you walk into the room where your mother is reading your diary as the adult you are now, with your older wiser self. What would you do to take care of your adolescent if you were able to walk in and see your mother doing that?

Polly: I could tell her this isn't appropriate and there's nothing wrong with this girl. She's a good kid. She did a few things that normal kids do, but very few that were bad. And there's nowhere to put her feelings in her real life, so she had to write her negative feelings in her diary. There's nothing wrong with her, and you're laying all your stuff onto her.

Margaret: Okay. So I'm going to stop you, Polly. One problem is that you're explaining: You are defending your adolescent instead of being firm with your mother. It doesn't sound like you know what that would look like. So I'd like to role-model that for you.

I'm you; I'm armed with my guidance. I walk in and I see my mother reading my diary. I would be outraged. I would say, "How dare you do that? You get away from that diary. That's none of your business. You have no right to read that. If you do it again, I'm calling Child Protective Services on you. Get out of here." Now what's the difference between what I did and what you did?

Polly: You put it on her that what she was doing was totally wrong.

Margaret: That's right, and that's what you would need to do as a loving adult. You couldn't do it as a child, but as an adult with your guidance, you're giving your inner child the message that you are not going to tolerate anything that's abusive. Then she starts to trust you.

Polly: I see that.

Margaret: You're an outraged adult, speaking out against injustice. This is the adult form of anger: outrage against injustice. The adult stands up and becomes ferocious for the inner child.

I assure you that if you practice going through various scenarios of abuse the way that I just did, your little girl will start to trust you. She'll start to believe that there really is a strong loving adult here who's going to take care of her, who's going to stand up for her and not allow anybody to abuse her again. Then she'll start to let you in on her feelings. Because the feelings from abuse are big, and you need a strong adult to manage them.

Polly: That makes sense.

Margaret: So how does that feel to you?

Polly: It feels good. I'm looking forward to trying that.

Margaret: Good! So take each incident that comes up for you. Redo it as a strong, fierce, loving adult. With situations of extreme abuse, you can even get yourself a bat and a pillow. You can hit the pillow and go after whoever was abusing you, because that will make your little girl feel so much safer.

Polly: I have a soft bat that I could do that with, but I've never done it.

Margaret: Well, try it, because your little girl will love to see you standing up for her and caring about her like that.

Polly: Yes.

Margaret: How are you feeling right now?

Polly: I feel good. That's sounds like a good idea. Thank you so much for that.

15

Communication in Relationships

One of the main issues concerning communication is that people have different ideas about what it is. To the wounded self, communication may seem like a demand. It may be expressing your feelings with the hope that somebody else will take responsibility for them and feel sorry for you. Communication may also be a way to control the other person, trying to make them stop doing something.

Although this is communication, it's not effective communication. Remember that the wounded self is all about control: That's why we created it in the first place. As little kids, we felt helpless, but we couldn't just feel helpless all the time, so we developed our wounded self to have control over getting love, avoiding pain, and feeling safe. What we communicate from our wounded self is all about that.

This is not effective communication. It will cause problems in relationships. Often a client will say, "I *am* communicating," but they're communicating from their wounded self. It's not working well, and it's never going to work well.

Communication from your loving adult, open to learning and connected with your guidance, is completely different. Now you're coming from a full place; you've taken care of yourself. You're not coming from a needy place; you're not coming from inner emptiness; you're not abandoning yourself. You're not making the other person responsible for you.

As a loving adult, one thing you're communicating is information, like, "I'm not going to be home until five o'clock." That's a communication. It's important in relationships just to let other people know what's happening.

Requests are another form of adult communication. As I've said, requests are different from demands. With a true request, a person may ask, "Would you be willing to do this?" But if you say, "No, I can't, I'm busy," the other person accepts it. There's no anger, no withdrawal.

Say you make a request and the other person doesn't agree to it. If you react with anger, withdrawal, or some other sort of punishment, it wasn't a request; it was a demand. That's not effective communication. We certainly have the right to make our requests, but we have to accept that we don't have control.

Then of course, there's the communication that's all about sharing love. This is such an important part of communicating: sharing what's in your heart, what's in your soul, sharing how you feel about this person and what you see as wonderful about this person—not to get anything back, not to be seen as a good person, but just to share what's in your heart. That creates a circle of love in relationships.

We can also share when we need help, like, "I'm feeling depressed today, and I don't know why. I need to talk about it for a few minutes to see if I can figure out what's going on for me. Can you talk with me about it?" That would be a communication: asking a partner to be there and listen to help you understand what's going on for yourself.

It's okay to share what's happening for you—not with an agenda to get the other person to do something about it, but to do something about it yourself and ask for some support.

It's important not to make a relationship therapeutic. If there's a lot going on with you, it's not healthy to try to turn your partner into your therapist. A loving relationship is not the same as a therapeutic relationship. If there's a lot going on that you need help with, seek out the help you need. Don't use your partner for that.

Nevertheless, we're here to support each other. When we're in a loving partnership, we have each other's back. Sometimes we're here just to let the other person vent. If that goes on a lot, you're probably not going to like it, but every once in a while, we may need to vent, and the other person may be fine with listening to and supporting us.

As you can see, there are many different forms of communication, but in every case, your intention will determine whether or not it's loving and effective. This is the basis of Inner Bonding: being aware of whether your intention is to control, avoid, and protect against pain—which is the wounded self—or to learn more about loving yourself and others.

Effective communication comes from the loving adult, from an intention to learn. Relationships, especially primary relationships, trigger everything that's unhealed in us; everything that we've never dealt with comes up. If we're open to learning with each other, it offers us an incredible arena for healing. We can help each other heal, not by being each other's therapists, but by being there to support each other, have each other's back.

Effective, loving communication leads to learning and growth, and eventually to intimacy and even fun. There is no intimacy, growth, passion, or fun without communication arising from a deep intention to learn. Effective communication from the loving adult is vital for a relationship to continue to be loving and alive.

The things that keep a relationship alive are learning, growing, and changing. If it were always the same, it would get boring and go dead. The loving adult wants to always be on this journey of learning and growing, which we can do with each other when we're both open to learning. True intimacy and the sharing of love is based on effective, loving communication from the loving adult with an intention to learn, grow, and become a more loving human being with yourself, others, and the planet.

Seeking a Beloved

Jessica: I've given myself up in relationships. I have a bit of history of that. But just last week, I said to myself, "Send me my beloved." All of a sudden, a fellow from our community garden asked me to have a chat and go for a walk. We seem to have some nice things in common, so we're going to go for a walk tomorrow.

Part of me gets very anxious about that. I left a relationship in 1999. I had certainly given myself up to that relationship, and I was sad to leave that. I've dated very seldom since then. I've done a lot of work, and maybe this is an opportunity to connect with a fellow human being and have a great experience. But part of me gets anxious that I'm not enough and I won't know what to say.

Dr. Margaret: Let's do some work with the anxiety. Take some deep breaths and use your breath to get present in your body with the anxiety. Where do you feel the anxiety?

Jessica: I think my heart. And then it comes up into my neck.

Dr. Margaret: So breathe into that. Sit with that for a moment. Sit with that little girl who's anxious, and decide that you want to take responsibility for that anxiety. Breathe into your heart, and open to learning. Invite the love, compassion, strength, and wisdom of your higher guidance into your heart.

Now you already know that you're telling your little girl that she's not enough or won't know what to say. Tune in, ask her if there's anything else you're telling her that's making her anxious.

Jessica: I think those are the two big things.

Dr. Margaret: I'd like you to go down into the wounded part of you who's telling her she's not enough and that she won't know what to say. How old is that wounded part?

Jessica: Six or seven.

Dr. Margaret: Now I'd like you to tune into that seven-year-old. Ask her what she is trying to control or avoid by telling your little girl that she's not enough and she's not going to know what to say.

Jessica: My sense is that I'm trying to keep myself safe. If I don't put myself out there, I won't have to be in a situation where I feel so inadequate.

Dr. Margaret: You are going to put yourself out there, you're going for a walk, but your wounded self is saying to your little girl that she's not good enough and she won't know what to say. Obviously, your wounded self is trying to create some safety. But how does that create safety in the eyes of your wounded self? How will that make you safe?

Jessica: If I don't say anything, I won't say the wrong thing.

Dr. Margaret: Your wounded self is saying that you're not good enough and you won't know what to say, so just be quiet and go along with everything he says. Right?

Jessica: Yeah.

Dr. Margaret: Your wounded self just wants to repeat what you've done in the past that she decided would make you feel safe. But it doesn't make your little girl feel safe. It makes her anxious. Notice that the anxiety is coming from your wounded self trying to make you safe, when all it's doing is creating anxiety.

Jessica: Right.

Dr. Margaret: Now, moving into step four, I want you to imagine being in a beautiful place in nature with your higher guidance and your little girl. I want you to ask your guidance, is it true that my soul essence, my true self, a spark of the divine within me is not good enough?

Jessica: No.

Dr. Margaret: Ask your higher guidance to show you some beautiful things about your little girl. What does your guidance see when looking at your little girl?

Jessica: She loves to run and jump and play and sing and just be herself. She's very sweet and she's friendly and natural and outgoing, likes playing with kids in the neighborhood and kickball and softball. She loves books, drawing pictures, and playing piano.

Dr. Margaret: As you look at her now, is there anything wrong with her?

Jessica: No.

Dr. Margaret: Is there anything not good enough about her?

Jessica: On that child level, no. Absolutely not.

Dr. Margaret: But don't think of her as a child. Think of her as your soul. Think of her as your true self. Because she's not really a child. We call our soul our inner child because it helps us remember to take responsibility for our feelings. But she's not a child. She's your immortal soul. She's who you really are. And you can see there's nothing wrong with who you are.

Jessica: There's nothing wrong with who I am.

Dr. Margaret: There is a lot wrong with the wounded self in all of us. The wounded self is a fabrication: We created it. Spirit created our true self, but we created our wounded self, so it's flawed. It's not good enough, and it won't know what to say. So when the wounded self says to your little girl, "You're not good enough, and you won't know what to say," she's really talking about herself, because she doesn't know about your true self.

Jessica: Oh!

Dr. Margaret: Now imagine being with this man on a walk. Instead of putting your wounded self in charge—who doesn't know what to say and who isn't good enough—what if you entered this conversation just to share who you are and find out about him? What if it wasn't to try to be safe? What if it had nothing to do with rejection? What if it was just about learning—sharing you and learning about him?

Jessica: Yes. I like that.

Dr. Margaret: What if it was about you showing up as an adult, holding your little girl's hand with one hand and holding the hand of your guidance with another hand so that you're full inside, ready to share who you are, rather than putting a seven-year-old in charge?

Jessica: I'm holding my inner child with one hand and my higher guidance with the other hand. My wounded self is out of the picture.

Dr. Margaret: That's right. Your wounded self is not in the picture at all. And as the adult, you decide on your intention. You decide that your intention is not to avoid rejection, because that's what creates the nervousness. Right?

Jessica: Yes.

Dr. Margaret: That's the agenda of the seven-year-old. You say to her, "You be quiet. I don't want you to be involved here, because my agenda is just to share who I am and get to know him."

Jessica: Yeah.

Dr. Margaret: How does that feel?

Jessica: That feels wonderful. Thank you very much for putting it into that crystal-clear perspective.

Dr. Margaret: When you think of it that way, can you be excited about it rather than nervous?

Jessica: Yes, absolutely.

16

Healing from an Abusive Relationship

When healing from an abusive relationship, first you need to be open to learning about your end of the system. However abusive it may have been, you tolerated this relationship for some good reasons—or at any rate, reasons that seemed good in the eyes of your wounded self.

You want to look at the ways that you abandoned yourself that allowed you to end up in an abusive relationship. Often if the other person is being abusive, you at the other end of it may be coming from a whole series of false beliefs. Did you believe that you deserved to be treated badly? Did you believe that it's your fault for causing somebody else to treat you that way? Did you believe that you could control your partner if only you were loving enough?

That's what I used to believe. My thirty-year marriage wasn't physically abusive, but it was emotionally abusive. I came from many false beliefs: If only I were loving enough, I could control my husband, and he would be the way I wanted him to be. If only I did everything right, if only I pleased him, if only I had enough sex with him or did everything he wanted me to do, he would love me the way I wanted to be loved. These were false beliefs, because we just don't have that control.

I gave my little girl over to my husband and he would act the way I wanted for a week or two. This happens very often in abusive relationships: They'll be fabulous for a day or a week or two and then go right back to the abuse.

Fortunately, when Inner Bonding came into my life, it showed me the way to heal. I learned to take 100 percent responsibility for my end of the system, for what I had ignored, for my covert controlling behavior. I wasn't a very overt controller. Often, the one at the receiving end of abuse is a covert controller, which means that you're trying to control by being compliant or maybe withdrawing at different times. It's not overt control, as when somebody gets angry or violent.

You can heal from an abusive relationship by doing your own inner work. It's important to be honest with yourself about your controlling behavior, which is often under the guise of compliance.

When I was being a compliant caretaker, I didn't know that it was a covert form of control. When you're being compliant, basically a martyr, it's easy to say, "Oh, look how loving I am." That's what I did. "Look how loving I am."

It was a shock to find out that that's not love. When we're abandoning ourselves, we really can't love another person. We're creating a hole inside, because we're not bringing love to ourselves, and that hole wants to get filled by somebody else's love. Then we have to try and control them.

That's why, when you're healing from an abusive relationship, it's important to see what your belief system is, how you are or were trying to control this person. You don't want to repeat this. You don't want to get into another abusive relationship, so now you need to do your healing work. Do your learning now. Do your Inner Bonding now. Find out how you have abandoned yourself. That's part of what Inner Bonding is about: learning to love yourself enough so that you're aware of what's happening with you and with somebody else in a relationship.

Anxiety in Relationships

Dan: I spoke with you a few months ago on anxiety within romantic relationships. Just reporting back that unfortunately, despite my efforts, my fear of loss did become a self-fulfilling prophecy, and that relationship is now over. I'd appreciate some help and support around this. If it's okay, I'll briefly outline a few details.

I became anxious, and nine times out of ten, I'd catch myself, and I would work with Inner Bonding and be able to contain myself. But there was that one time out of ten when I became anxious, and I reacted by trying to get some reassurance from my partner in ways that must have felt quite smothering to her—perhaps almost like an attack of sorts. She has had a difficult upbringing and is facing challenging life circumstances at the moment. I just don't think she was able to hold my anxiety alongside everything else in her life.

This was followed by a slow breakup process. After a certain event, she began to withdraw more and more, and it's gotten to a point now where we're taking space; we're not in regular contact. I'm currently processing and experiencing a lot of shock. It feels like a bad dream that things suddenly fell apart. I feel regret and self-blame, wishing that I could have done things differently.

I'm still deeply infatuated with her, and I'm experiencing a lot of separation anxiety and heartbreak, which can be very overwhelming in the body. I'm doing my best to work through it and use this as an opportunity to grow. But at the same time, my wounded self is sometimes screaming thoughts telling me that I can't live without her; I want to die. It leads to tears and panic attacks, and I would appreciate some help in working with this.

Dr. Margaret: Take some deep breaths, please. Just breathe into that anxiety, that panic, which is obviously coming from self-abandonment and putting your wounded self in charge. Breathe into your heart, open to learning, and invite your higher guidance in.

I'd like you to ask your guidance for help right now in tuning into why you don't want responsibility for making your inner child feel safe and secure. There are some false beliefs here. You're going to need your guidance to tune into them. You don't want to be the loving adult; you don't want to be the one to take care of your little boy. You handed him away to your partner. You said you needed her to reassure him, you need her to make him feel safe. This suggests that you think that it's a woman's responsibility to make your little boy feel safe and secure rather than your own responsibility as a loving adult. There's some good reason that you don't want this responsibility. See if you can tune into what that is for you. There's some big resistance here. What comes up for you? Don't overthink.

Dan: Yeah. It's too hard and I can't be bothered.

Dr. Margaret: How old is the part of you that says it's too hard and you can't be bothered?

Dan: About five.

Dr. Margaret: It is too hard for a five-year-old. It's not the job of a five-year-old, right? So to give it to a five-year-old, to give it to your wounded self, will always lead to problems in a relationship. But you're not five. For some good reason, you as the adult don't want the responsibility for your five-year-old, for making yourself feel safe, secure, and loved.

Dan: What comes to mind is a sense of not knowing how, of not having a blueprint for how that would feel. Not even knowing how to.

Dr. Margaret: In Inner Bonding, how do we learn how?

Dan: We ask spirit?

Dr. Margaret: That's right. Very few of us know how; few of us were given role modeling for how to be loving to ourselves. I certainly wasn't. You don't know how, but you can learn how by opening to learning with your guidance and asking what's loving to you in any given moment.

But there's some deeper issue going on here; there's some resistance to that. There's something here about that it's not your job or that it's a woman's job, not yours. See if you can tune into anything like that inside.

Dan: I'm sensing a resentment toward my emotionally absent mother.

Dr. Margaret: It was her job when you were a child, but is it her job now?

Dan: Oh, no. I'm referring to when I was younger, of course.

Dr. Margaret: Okay. But we're talking about right now. Right now, it sounds like you're still stuck blaming your mother for not being there in the way that you wanted, but still you are not being willing to be the loving mother and father that your inner child needs now. There's some resistance for you to show up that way with your guidance. What do you think that's about for you?

Dan: That I'm bad.

Dr. Margaret: That you're bad? Well, that gets you off the hook, doesn't it? If your wounded self is telling you you're bad, why would you love yourself? But isn't that a way to avoid responsibility?

There's something deeper that you need to take a look at, because you are willing to lose your relationship rather than learn to be a loving adult. Even feeling your anxiety but managing it—that's not what Inner Bonding is. Feeling your anxiety is about learning what you're doing to abandon yourself, and you weren't doing that. Then at some point you made your partner responsible, which you were doing all along anyway. Whether you did it overtly or not, I'm sure she could feel the pull from you telling her she's supposed to be the caring one, the giving one. How come you're not supposed to be the one to do that for yourself and share that with her?

Dan: It's funny, I actually feel a need to defend myself. I know that I was supportive of her. But that's just defending my self-image.

Dr. Margaret: Yes. But if you are abandoning yourself, the support you're giving her could have also felt like a pull. Because if you're not coming from a full place, if you're not coming from a place filled up with love when you're being supportive of her, there's an agenda. There's an agenda saying that then she'll give you back whatever you want. That's what caretakers do. They'll give to get something back.

When there's an agenda in the giving, it doesn't feel like giving to the other person. And if you're abandoning yourself, there's always an agenda in the giving. There's no such thing as being able to give from a full loving heart when you're abandoning yourself. I encourage you to continue to look a little deeper as to why in your mind it is not your responsibility to make you feel loved and safe and full and worthy. Why isn't it your responsibility?

Dan: Is there even a belief behind it, or is it just a pattern of avoiding that I just need to consciously make the choice to address?

Dr. Margaret: There is a belief behind it. There's a false belief behind it that would be important for you to come to terms with. Many men grow up with a belief that women are naturally more caring, more motherly, and more giving; therefore, in a relationship, it's their responsibility to do that for you. I don't know if you have that or not, but there's something in there. You handed your little boy to her for some reason. Why did you hand your little boy to her?

Dan: I wanted to feel loved.

Dr. Margaret: Yes. And it's her responsibility, not yours, according to your belief system. You were abandoning yourself. You were not loving yourself, so you wanted her to make you feel loved. But there's some reason that you don't think it's your responsibility to love yourself and share love rather than to get love. Your intention was to get love, not to share love. Do you believe that you're not capable, that a woman is capable and you're not, or that somebody else is more capable than you of bringing love to yourself, or that you're not capable of connecting with a source of love? You made her your higher power. Is there something in the way in your mind of you having your own higher power?

Dan: By default, I'd say yes. Like not having the belief that I have the capability that it's even possible.

Dr. Margaret: So that really gets you off the hook.

Dan: Yeah.

Dr. Margaret: Why would you not be capable of opening to your higher power? Why would you not be capable of that?

Dan: Unwillingness to feel pain?

Dr. Margaret: That may be the answer here. You might want to go a little deeper into that unwillingness, because if you're unwilling to feel pain, you can't love. If you're unwilling to feel pain, then your wounded self is always in charge, causing pain.

Pain is a teacher. If you're unwilling to feel pain, you can't see what you're doing that's causing it. You can't deal with the pain of life or connect to your guidance, because your frequency would be too low if you're expending your energy avoiding pain. If your intention is to avoid pain, your wounded self is always in charge. So what is it about pain? Why are you unwilling to experience pain? It seems to me it's putting you in pain all the time. What's the fear of pain?

Dan: I'll be completely lost and adrift and consumed by it.

Dr. Margaret: For a three-year-old, yes. I want you to open up to your guidance and ask if that's true if you're willing to show up as an adult.

Dan: Yeah, but it feels like unfamiliar territory.

Dr. Margaret: This is going to be your challenge. You have a lot of pain right now. I want to encourage you to practice opening to your guidance, bringing that love inside and bringing it down to your little boy, who is in pain. You think he's in pain because of your partner leaving, but I think he's in pain because you abandoned him. I think that's the primary pain—not that there's not some heartbreak of your partner leaving, but I think the real pain in you is from self-abandonment. I want to encourage you to open to the pain, bring love inside, and explore what you're doing to cause the pain instead of focusing on the relationship. Are you willing to do that?

Dan: Yes.

17

Moving Past Social Phobia

Many people experience phobia in social situations. If this is the case with you, you can use Inner Bonding to heal social phobia.

To begin, when you think about being afraid in social situations, see if you can tune into how old you were when it started to happen. When did you start being afraid? Was it as a child? Was it as an adolescent? Was it as a young adult? When did you start feeling afraid?

Also see if you can tune into what you're afraid of. Usually when people have social phobia, they're afraid of being rejected. They're afraid of being judged, ridiculed, laughed at, or humiliated in some way. That frequently links back to experiences in the family and especially in school. Many people had traumatic experiences in school—being left out, laughed at, humiliated, rejected.

When you are afraid in social situations, it means that there's no loving adult present. You're operating as that traumatized child or adolescent, afraid of what happened to you when you were younger.

Healing from social phobia is about developing your loving adult rather than going into a social situation as a child or adolescent. It's about going in as a spiritually connected, loving adult so that you're not saying things to your inner child like, "You better not mess up" or "People have to like you" or "Oh my God, we're going to get laughed at." The loving adult never says those things. Those are things the wounded self says. They scare your inner child and cause social phobia.

Imagine that you have an actual child who is going to a birthday party. You say to the child, "You'd better say everything right. You'd better do everything right. You'd better not make a fool of yourself. People had better like you. If they don't, you're not good enough." How would the child feel? Of course, the child would feel scared. The child would probably clam up and be immobilized, afraid to say the wrong thing.

But say that child has been taught that who they are is wonderful and lovable, and they know that no matter what happens, their mom and dad are going to love them and their worth does not depend on what happens at the party. In that case, they're going to go in with confidence. Children can learn at a very young age to speak up for themselves, refusing to tolerate any abusive behavior.

A mother I was working with had a seven-year-old daughter. She came home and said that one of the boys was bullying her at school. The mother said, "Well, what did you do?" The daughter said, "I said to him, 'I know that you're a really nice person underneath, and I know you're acting this way because somebody's hurting you at home. It really has nothing to do with me, and I feel sorry for you,' and I walked away." The daughter knew that it wasn't about her, because she had loving parents who helped her know and see herself.

That's your job on the inner level. It's the responsibility of you as a loving adult to do your Inner Bonding work so that when you're in a social situation, your little girl or boy doesn't feel alone or scared. He or she will know that if somebody is being mean or rejecting or laughing at you, your loving adult will speak up and disengage from that person. Your adult won't take it personally—meaning that there's something wrong with you—because it has nothing to do with you.

When people act that way, they're projecting their own self-rejection onto others. They're being hurtful because of their self-abandonment. That's what people do when they are operating out of their wounded self: They project their self-loathing out onto other people. They make fun of them. They try to humiliate them.

A loving adult would never do that and would never take that personally. The loving adult would say to the inner child, "Oh dear, this person is operating out of their wounded self, and they're dumping their self-loathing onto us. It has nothing to do with you, sweetie. I'm right here. It's not about you. You're wonderful, and I love you, and spirit's here. We're being surrounded by love. I'm just going to walk away from this person. I'm not going to put you in the line of fire. I'm not going to let you take it personally, because you're a lovable and beautiful little girl or boy." The inner child will feel safe because you are there as a spiritually connected, loving adult.

That is what it takes to get over social phobia. It takes a devoted Inner Bonding practice to develop your loving adult. If you have social phobia, I hope you'll recognize that whenever you're feeling scared, it's because you're not showing up as a loving adult. You're abandoning yourself.

I've had to work hard on this. I've never had social phobia, but social situations have not been easy for me, because I'm introverted. I tend to be shy and quiet, and I've had to learn to be fine with that. It took work in developing my loving adult to be okay with not being extroverted and out there, always knowing what to say.

Now I value my introversion and my quietness. Even my shyness is fine with me. I just let myself be who I am and I speak when it's important to me to do that. I don't compare myself to other people anymore, which I used to do all the time. I don't judge myself or take other people's behavior personally, so I don't feel any fear in social situations.

Retraumatizing

Faith: I have these poems I've written. People like them, and I don't share them. Maybe social phobia is holding me back.

Dr. Margaret: Let's do some work on that. Take some deep breaths into the fear of sharing your poems. Where do you feel the fear in your body?

Faith: I'm feeling it right now in my chest.

Dr. Margaret: Breathe into your chest and get present with the fear. Move toward it, welcome it, embrace it. Make a decision: You want responsibility for it—that you want to know what it's telling you. Breathe into your heart, and open to learning. Visualize your higher guidance, your higher self. Invite love and compassion and strength and wisdom and courage and truth into your heart, breathing that in, making sure you're really open, making sure that you really want to learn, that you're really curious.

Go into the fear. Go back into the fear and ask your little girl what your wounded self is telling her that's scaring her from putting out your writing.

Faith: When you speak of the higher power, I identify with that. And all of a sudden, I just feel empowered.

Dr. Margaret: Great, but please just follow what I'm asking you to do. Please ask your little girl what you're telling her that's scaring her.

Faith: When I go into my feelings, what comes up is terror.

Dr. Margaret: Faith, there's something you're telling your inner child right now. What are you telling her that's terrifying her?

Faith: She's no good.

Dr. Margaret: Okay. So how old is the wounded self that's telling her she's no good?

Faith: I have two, and they're split. The little girl before six was saying, "This is impossible. I can't stay here." Then the little girl after six was saying, "This is a nightmare." It's kind of a shift. I don't know how to explain it.

Dr. Margaret: Let's assume that you have a six-year-old wounded part inside. When you want to put out your writing, it's telling your little girl, "No, no, because you're no good." Then what will happen? What is your wounded self telling her will happen if you put your writing out?

Faith: She's going to be shamed, blamed.

Dr. Margaret: Yeah. So she'll be shamed. She'll be blamed like you were as a child, right?

Faith: Yes.

Dr. Margaret: The wounded six-year-old is saying, "No, no. We can't risk putting this out, because the world is just like our parents. They're going to shame and blame us, and it's not worth it." Of course that would terrify the child. Why would anybody want to put themselves in that position? But do you think that your six-year-old really knows whether that's true or not?

Faith: That's what happened. That's not today.

Dr. Margaret: That's right. Do you think your six-year-old has access to what's true today?

Faith: Wow! No.

Dr. Margaret: Now I want you to imagine that you're in a beautiful place in nature, sitting at a picnic table. Imagine sitting with an older, wiser part of you, your own higher self—500 years older than you are right now. Very wise, loving, powerful. Ask her if it's true that your six-year-old knows what she's talking about that if you put your writing out, you're going to be shamed and blamed.

Faith: No! My guidance is telling me that it would be loving to me to publish my poetry, which is what my friends have been telling me.

Dr. Margaret: Obviously, there's trauma there in your inner child's growing-up years. The problem is that until you develop a loving adult, you can't heal the trauma.

This is true for all of us. If you continue to treat yourself the way that you were treated—if the wounded self continues to tell her little girl that she's not good enough—that's retraumatizing. If she continues to tell her little girl that if she puts out her writing that she's going to be shamed and blamed, that's retraumatizing. So she's retraumatizing herself. Whenever you're abandoning yourself, you're retraumatizing yourself.

I work with clients who have done many forms of trauma therapy, like the Emotional Freedom Technique, Trauma Release Exercises, Somatic Experiencing, and EMDR (Eye movement desensitization and reprocessing). There are many forms of therapy for releasing old trauma out of the body. Yet I've seen many clients who have gone through many trauma therapies but are still traumatized. These trauma therapies are excellent, but they are not enough by themselves. I recommend them as adjunct therapies along with Inner Bonding. If you are also not practicing Inner Bonding, developing your loving adult and healing your false beliefs, you might continue to retraumatize yourself.

If you're not practicing Inner Bonding alongside these trauma therapies, you're going to keep abandoning yourself, and self-abandonment is retraumatizing. I encourage all the trauma therapies—whatever works for any given person—along with Inner Bonding.

18

Feeling Your Feelings

I've been asked, how do you feel your feelings when you're processing and letting go of difficult experiences? Difficult situations create painful feelings. What you want to do is *not* avoid the feelings. You want to feel the feelings with gentleness. You want to get really present with your feelings, and you want to be compassionate with them.

Of course, things happen externally over which we have no control and which bring up the existential pain of life. In those cases, it's not a matter of letting go of the situation; it's a matter of going inside with compassion, holding your heart, letting your inner child know that he or she isn't alone, and bringing in the love of spirit. It's a matter of staying with the feelings with compassion until they are ready to move through you—for that time. In particularly painful situations, such as loss of a loved one, the feelings will come up over and over, and each time you need to hold them with love and compassion.

If it's a situation such as a conflict, it's important to open to learning about our participation in the situation. Are we taking care of ourselves? Are we being reactive? Did we go to our wounded self? Are we trying to control the situation?

You start with your feelings. If it's an external situation over which you have no control, you want to be in deep compassion and connection with your guidance. If it's a situation where your feelings are wounded, go through an Inner Bonding process. The more you learn, the more the difficult situation may start to get resolved, if it's possible for it to be resolved.

Recently some clients of mine had to put down their beloved dog. That's a difficult situation. It's not a matter of letting go of the situation; it's a matter of feeling the heartbreak over losing a beloved pet. That's step one of Inner Bonding: being present in your body with your feelings and taking compassionate responsibility for them, whether they're the feelings of your wounded self or the painful feelings of life that are being caused by an external person or situation.

Jealousy and the Wounded Self

Tia: For me this topic pops up a difficult situation for me, which is jealousy. I can see that I abandon myself and cannot really feel my value. It's like I get stuck in the process.

Dr. Margaret: I would very much like to be of help to you. What kind of situation triggers your jealousy?

Tia: I'm in a relationship where I have this tendency of being jealous. I have a constant fear of my partner wanting to be with someone else.

Dr. Margaret: Think of a recent time when you felt jealous, take some deep breaths into the feeling of jealousy, and get present with it. Make a decision that you want to learn more about this feeling and that you want to take responsibility for it. You want to learn what you're doing to cause it.

Now breathe into your heart and open to learning. Visualize your higher guidance, and invite love and compassion and strength and wisdom and courage and truth into your heart. Breathing that in, making sure that you're really curi-

Feeling Your Feelings

ous. You really do want to understand what you're doing to cause it.

Now breathe back down into the jealousy and ask your little girl what you're telling her from your wounded self. How are you treating her that makes her feel so insecure, that makes her feel scared he's going to want somebody else? What are you telling her? How are you treating her? What are you doing or not doing that makes your little girl feel so insecure and jealous? Then go inside and let that jealous part of you, the little girl who's feeling jealous, answer.

Tia: It comes up very strongly like criticism.

Dr. Margaret: That you're criticizing yourself?

Tia: Yes. And afraid of being criticized. A lot of fear and sadness comes up.

Dr. Margaret: But what are you telling yourself that creates the fear and sadness?

Tia: Telling myself that I'm stupid. It's like I can hear it; it feels like my father's voice, actually.

Dr. Margaret: Okay, good. So your wounded self has absorbed your father's voice, right?

Tia: Uh-huh.

Dr. Margaret: And what did your father say?

Tia: Really harsh criticism, like, "Are you stupid? You can't do it like that." And always telling me I'm doing wrong.

Dr. Margaret: How old do you think you were when you absorbed your father's critical voice and started treating yourself that way?

Tia: Maybe four.

Dr. Margaret: Okay. Imagine you have a four-year-old wounded part of you who has absorbed your father's criticisms and who tells your little girl you're stupid; you're not good enough; you're not doing it right; what's wrong with you?

That's going to make you feel very insecure, isn't it? It's going to make you feel like you're not as good as other women.

So when your partner spends time with a friend or talks to another woman, that four-year-old goes right into action, doesn't she? Telling your little girl, "This woman is better than you are; you're stupid; you're not good enough. You don't do things right." That's going to create a lot of fear and jealousy, isn't it? (She nods.) Of course it does. When you're telling yourself those lies, it's going to make you feel bad.

Now I want you to imagine being in a beautiful place in nature, a place you love to be in, sitting at a picnic table with your higher guidance. I want you to imagine that your little girl is there too.

First, I want you to ask your guidance to show you some things that are beautiful and wonderful about your little girl, and why somebody might love her, because your guidance loves her. What does your guidance see when she looks at who you are in your soul?

Tia: She's a very warm and caring person.

Dr. Margaret: Good. What else?

Tia: When she feels safe, she is playful and happy and shining.

Dr. Margaret: So that's who she really is, right? Ask, is it true that she's stupid and wrong and not good enough?

Tia: No, but it's like it pops up that I'm not good enough.

Dr. Margaret: Yes, that's what you absorbed from your father. But if you're a loving, caring, warm, playful person when you feel safe, what's not good enough about you? What actually isn't good enough?

Tia: That I hide, that I'm afraid to show myself. It's like I withdraw.

Dr. Margaret: But that's your wounded self. Your wounded self has learned to protect and control and avoid and tell your little girl lies. But we're looking at your little girl, your soul, your essence, the spark of the divine within you, and your guidance said she's a warm, caring, playful person, right? I'm talking about that. That's your essence. That's your true self. Is there anything wrong with your true self?

Tia: No.

Dr. Margaret: Right! Nobody's wounded self is lovable. We're not lovable when we're being in our wounded self. Nobody likes our wounded self. But that's not who you are. Your partner didn't fall in love with your wounded self. Your partner fell in love with your essence. Your partner fell in love with your warmth and your caring and your playfulness and all the wonderful things about you.

When we connect with somebody and choose to partner up, it's because we value who they are in their essence. We don't like their wounded self. Nobody likes anybody's wounded self. But we value who this person is in their essence. And we're each unique in our essence, which means that your partner values who you are as a soul, and that who you are is unique and not easily replaced.

We're not replaceable because we're not all the same. We're all very different. We're all unique expressions of the divine, which means that he could talk to however many women he wants, but they're not you. You're the one he is with. You're the one he fell in love with. You're the one he's chosen. But if you act out of your wounded self enough, you push him away. If you act out the jealousy, you push him away, because that's not you. That's your wounded self, and wounded selves destroy relationships.

Tia: Yes, I've been there.

Dr. Margaret: One thing that would be loving to you is—when he's out with somebody else or talking to another woman, or whatever it is that's triggering you—to go to your guidance and ask to see who you are in your essence and start to value it

You're treating yourself like your father did. You're not treating yourself like a loving Mom and Dad. You're not seeing who you really are. You're not telling your little girl, "You're such a sweet, warm, caring person. Of course your partner loves you. You're fun, you're playful." That would be the truth. Instead you're treating your little girl like your father did: "You're stupid. What's the matter with you? You're not good enough." That's what's causing the jealousy.

Tia: Yes, I see that.

Dr. Margaret: It's about your intention. When you're treating yourself that way, your intention is to control. You want to control him by judging yourself.

Tia: I can also see that I'm probably trying to control him by being caring or loving as well.

Dr. Margaret: The wounded self can control through caretaking. It's not really loving. It's not loving to give to somebody in order to control them.

But your guidance said that your soul is loving and caring. Again, it's about your intention. If your intention is to be loving to yourself, then you can share your love with him. If your intention is to control him, you can do it by acting out your jealousy, being angry, being overly nice, giving yourself up, or acting loving. Those are all forms of control, but none of them work well, because we don't control love. And none of them are loving to you.

One thing that I find really helpful is mirroring. When you see yourself behaving in a way that you value, you say it out loud to your little girl. If I'm in my art studio and doing something that I love, I'll say to my little girl, "Thank you so much. I love your creativity. I feel so blessed by your creativity." Or I might say to her after a session, "I so appreciate your perceptiveness. I so appreciate your ability to see more deeply into things. Thank you so much for that." I'm constantly mirroring and thanking my soul for who she is.

I didn't use to do that. I used to do what you do: "You're not good enough. What's the matter with you? You shouldn't have said that." I had critical parents, and of course I incorporated those qualities of theirs.

I want to encourage you to notice these beautiful qualities of your soul and comment on them instead of letting your wounded self say to your little girl that she's stupid and not good enough. That's hurtful, very unloving to you. How are you feeling right now?

Tia: It feels like light—open and light in my heart. Like that I have space now, and I feel happy and excited.

Dr. Margaret: Good for you. Thank you for working with me on that.

19

Staying Centered

How do you stay centered when you're getting triggered? Being triggered means that your wounded self has been activated in some way. You feel unseen, unheard, angry, afraid. You're being triggered into the usual patterns your wounded self has learned to control, protect, or avoid. We've learned many ways to react when these fears and feelings are triggered, such as anger, blaming, explaining, defending, arguing, debating, complying, withdrawing, resisting.

Obviously, it's a challenge to stay centered in these circumstances, and it isn't going to happen all at once. The way to learn to stay centered is to have a consistent Inner Bonding practice, because that's what develops the loving adult. We're not going to stay centered if we can't turn to our loving adult, connected with our higher guidance, and ask for guidance in the moment. That's what it means to stay centered—to be able to ask in that moment, "What's my highest good right now?" It takes a lot of practice to remember to ask, because it's automatic for most of us to react to any kind of attack, blame, or withdrawal of love.

Your fear of rejection and your fear of engulfment are the two principal fears that get you off-center. If you feel that somebody's trying to control you and you're fearful of losing yourself, you might pull back, withdraw, shut down, or resist. Or if you fear being rejected, you might react with compliance or explaining. It's either the fear of loss of self or the fear of loss of the other person that might trigger you. When the fear of loss of the other person is triggered, you're going to want to change their mind. You're going to want to control them by saying or doing what you imagine is the right thing.

That's what the wounded self is all about. It's about trying to have control over getting love, avoiding pain, and feeling safe from being controlled, engulfed, or rejected. Because we've all practiced our protective controlling responses for so many years, it's naturally easy to go into our learned programmed protections when somebody is triggering our fears. It's a big challenge in that moment to keep from going into the programmed wounded self while staying in your heart, staying open to learning, and asking, "What is loving to me right now?" That's what it means to be centered.

There are two levels to be aware of in any communication: the issue and how the issue is dealt with. Say somebody is mad at you for forgetting something at the market or being late. That's the issue, the level of content. Then there's how the issue is being dealt with. This is the deeper level, the level of intent. Because we are so programmed to respond to content, it's hard to remember that if somebody is doing something that's triggering you, they're likely in their wounded self. And if you're addressing content when somebody's in their wounded self, you're not going to get anywhere, because neither of you is open. We can't be open and closed at the same time.

As a result, addressing content—defending yourself, explaining, telling them why you did or didn't do what you did—isn't going to get anywhere. It's a waste of energy and a waste of time because the other person is closed.

You might also get triggered because of your own self-judgments. Somebody might ask with true curiosity and no blame, "How come you forgot this at the market?" On the face of it, it's a reasonable question. If you're triggered, it's not necessarily because of the other person but because of your own self-judgment—in which case you're stuck in your wounded self.

There's no way to talk about the issue if one or both of you are in your wounded self. If this is the case, say something like, "I'm getting triggered right now. I need to calm down. I'll come back in fifteen minutes, and we'll try to talk about it then." It's best not to get into an argument if your wounded self is triggered.

If somebody's in their wounded self and you are able to stay in your loving adult, I've found that there are only a few loving responses that your guidance will give you. Maybe they're scared. If so, reach out and give comfort: "It's okay, I'm here. I want to listen. I want to understand."

Another is to consciously be open to learning: "There must be a good reason you're upset. I'm listening to you. I really want to understand what's so upsetting to you." If you think the other person isn't going to open, the third response is to say, "I don't think we're going to get anywhere right now. Let's just take a break." Usually it'll take fifteen minutes to a half hour for the energy of the wounded self to go down; then you might be able to come back together and talk about the issue with openness.

But both people have to be open. If you come back feeling open and compassionate but the other person isn't, you have to leave it alone and come back in another half hour. Or you can say, "Let me know when you feel up to talking about this." In any event, you won't get anywhere if one or both of you are in your wounded selves. When we get triggered, it's challenging to remember that we can be a loving adult, that we can open to our guidance.

As we've seen, it's vitally important in Inner Bonding to be connected to your higher guidance. This leads to the question of how to stay connected.

It's one thing to connect when you're alone. It's another to connect when you're around people, which is much more challenging, especially if you're in a relationship where the fear of losing others—or losing ourselves—comes up. Many people will automatically go into their protective controlling behavior, their wounded selves.

Of course, all of that lowers your frequency. So the bottom line in being able to connect with your guidance is keeping your frequency high. Many factors come into play here.

One huge effect on frequency comes from what you put in your body. Anything that's not right for your body is going to lower your frequency. Of course, processed or factory-farmed foods, sugar, and addictive substances lower your frequency. So does breathing bad air or drinking chlorinated water. There are many ways of absorbing toxins: your makeup, your cologne, your perfume, or your hairspray. If you really want to stay in a high frequency, you need to be vigilant about what you eat and what you expose yourself to.

But the main thing in keeping your frequency high is your intention. When you're alone but your intention is to not feel alone, you might turn to various ways of avoiding your feelings, and you won't be able to connect with your guidance.

Any intention to avoid or protect against pain lowers our frequency. Again, it comes down to vigilance—in this case, about your intention. Since virtually all of us learn to control, avoid, and protect against pain, you have to maintain a conscious process of staying in step one of Inner Bonding so that you're aware of your feelings. Your feelings will tell you the moment you've abandoned yourself. If you don't pay attention to them, you're likely to fall into the trap of protecting with various addictive behaviors, and your frequency will go down.

Although it's easier to be open to your connection when you're alone, you also need to maintain your frequency in the presence of others. Most people have learned to try to have control over getting approval, validation, and love. This intention to *get* something lowers your frequency. You won't be able to maintain your frequency around other people when your intention is to get love rather than give love and share love, and you won't be able to do this if you're abandoning yourself, and unless you've decided that you're willing for them to be upset with you or even to lose them in order to stay connected with yourself and not lose yourself.

When you learn to stay connected with your guidance around others, your relationships will change. Everything will start to feel different. Now, instead of coming from your wounded self trying to get something, you already have it: You're already connected with your guidance. You're already full of love, you already approve of and validate yourself, and you don't need anything from the other person. When you reach this place, it's easy to stay connected with your guidance.

I frankly don't know of anything more important or fulfilling than staying connected with my guidance. I am highly motivated to do everything I can regarding the air I breathe, what I put in my body, and my intention around people. I make a conscious choice to stay in my intention to learn about what's loving to me. If you practice this, then over time, you're able to connect with your guidance more and more of the time. You're able to access moment by moment guidance of what's loving to you in any situation. After you've spent some time practicing Inner Bonding and dealing with your false beliefs, the energy of the wounded self gets smaller and smaller until you barely hear its voice.

As I've already pointed out, the wounded self is in the lower left brain. It's built in; it's the fight-or-flight mechanism. We need it. We need to be able to react rapidly if there's a threat to our physical being. It's not going to go away, but as you develop your spiritually connected, loving adult, you will no longer react to ordinary stresses with the fight-or-flight responses of the wounded self. Eventually, you feel safer and the wounded self gives up trying to control, because it realizes that you, as an adult connected with your guidance, do a much better job of keeping you safe. In fact, the wounded self is incapable of keeping you safe. But the more you practice Inner Bonding and develop your strong, loving, spiritually connected adult, the more you will naturally access your guidance throughout the day, the safer you feel, and the quieter your wounded self becomes.

That's what happens when you consistently practice staying present in your body in step one of Inner Bonding. You know the moment you're feeling anything less than peace and fullness inside. You can then do an Inner Bonding process and get your frequency back up and into connection.

People sometimes say that when they ask their higher guidance a question, they don't feel that they get a clear answer.

Higher guidance can take many forms. It can be a voice, it can be a feeling, it can be images, it can be in dreams, it can be something you hear yourself saying to somebody else or something somebody else says to you. It can be in a book. Guidance finds many ways to communicate with you.

If you feel you're not receiving information, you need to look to your frequency. Either you're not truly in an intention to learn and the wounded self is pretending to be open, or your body is not clear. You're putting food in your body that's keeping your frequency low. Or both your intent and your food are keeping your frequency too low to access your guidance. Accessing higher guidance is about our frequency, which includes both our intention and what's happening in our physical body.

The six steps of Inner Bonding are a pathway for learning to stay connected with your spiritual guidance throughout the day. As I said, there's nothing better than that. It makes me feel safe to know that I'm always being guided, that I have the choice to stay open, and that spirit is always here watching out for me, letting me know what I need to attend to. That deep sense of safety and faith comes about as you practice Inner Bonding. I strongly encourage you to build that practice into your life.

Vanquishing Depression

Monica: I'm feeling very depressed at the moment.

Dr. Margaret: Let's work with that. I want you to take some deep breaths into the depression. Where do you feel the depression?

Monica: In my heart.

Dr. Margaret: Breathe into that. Get present with it, present with the heaviness, the sadness. Make a decision that you want responsibility for it, and breathe into your heart, open to learning, and visualize your higher guidance.

Monica: My higher guidance feels very far away.

Dr. Margaret: I want you to visualize an older, wiser aspect of you, who as your higher soul is right here, can't go away, is a part of you, with you, and all around you. It's you. It's a higher aspect of you. Invite the love and compassion and strength and wisdom of your higher self into your heart.

Now go back in, and I'd like you to ask that little girl inside who is depressed what you've been telling her, how you've been treating her, what you've been doing or not doing, that's making her feel depressed. Then go inside and let the depression speak.

Monica: I feel like I'm never going to make any changes in my life, and I feel completely powerless to try and change it.

Dr. Margaret: So you have a wounded part that says, "We'll never make any changes; we are powerless to change our life." Is that right?

Monica: Yes. At night, I wake up feeling really terrified because I know my wounded self has kicked in. I find it really hard to dislodge it and move into higher guidance.

Dr. Margaret: Of course it is very depressing to your little girl that your wounded self is in charge, saying you're powerless, you can't do anything, you're stuck.

Monica: Yeah.

Dr. Margaret: Depression is the way your little girl communicates with you. You see, those feelings—anxiety, depression, guilt, shame, anger—are letting us know that there's a lie happening. The wounded self always lies, because it has no access to the truth. Let's go a little deeper to the part of you that's saying, "We can't change anything; we're powerless." How old is that part?

Monica: Five.

Dr. Margaret: What was happening at five?

Monica: I'm being ignored.

Dr. Margaret: Ignored by your parents? Okay, so as a five-year-old, you were powerless over them.

Monica: I was.

Dr. Margaret: You're powerless over them, but also, as a five-year-old, you don't have a lot of power over yourself. It's not like you can say, "I don't want to be in this family. I'm going to go to another family." You don't have a whole lot of power when you're five.

But it sounds like you've put a five-year-old in charge, and she's telling your little girl the lie that it's the same as it was when you were five. That's very depressing. It's a lie, because you're not five and you're not powerless. You're still powerless over others, but not over yourself.

Monica: Yeah.

Dr. Margaret: But let's see if you can open up to your higher self. Imagine yourself in a beautiful place in nature, and you're sitting there with your older, wiser self, your higher self. Ask, is it true that I'm powerless over myself?

Monica: No.

Dr. Margaret: So what is the truth?

Monica: I do have the power.

Dr. Margaret: I'd like to hear what changes you'd like to make that your wounded self says you can't make.

Monica: I desperately want to change my work. I'm in this trap of earning enough money to live off but never reaching a profit margin that I can invest in further training. I've done lots of online work, but I'm not earning enough.

Dr. Margaret: What is your work?

Monica: I work in conflict resolution and mediation, so I work with organizations and help them resolve conflicts. But I'm in this trap of working to earn just enough to pay the rent and the bills. I get scared because I'm single, I don't have children, and I'm moving on in age.

Dr. Margaret: Do you like your work?

Monica: To a degree. I'd much rather work in energy medicine, and I've invested in a bioresonance machine. But I'm finding it difficult to do all the work I do to live and build that career up as well. I get exhausted, and I end up feeling like I can't make any changes.

Dr. Margaret: I get the feeling that you're not keeping your frequency high enough to stay connected to your guidance so that you can manifest. It's the law of attraction: like attracts like. Depression is a very low frequency. Telling yourself you have no power is a very low frequency. You're putting your wounded self in charge.

When I asked you to connect with your guidance, you said, "My guidance is very far away." You can't manifest that way. We manifest when we're connected, when we're with our guidance, when we're listening to ourselves and taking good care of ourselves, when we're showing up as a loving adult, when we're eating well and keeping the frequency of our body high. Then we co-create with spirit. But if you do anything that lowers your frequency, you're sabotaging yourself. You're letting your wounded self be in charge and tell you you're powerless, which is a lie. You're not five, and you're not powerless over your manifestation.

People do many things that lower their frequency. One of my clients realized that she had gotten into smoking pot in the evenings, and her motivation and manifestation went down. When I was working with her, I said, "Your energy and frequency are so low." When she stopped smoking pot, suddenly all her motivation and energy came back.

Different people react differently to various substances. Some people can smoke pot and it doesn't affect them that way, but many people's bodies don't react well to things like that, or even to specific foods. Some people might be able to eat certain foods that other people can't. In any case, one thing you are doing to lower your frequency is putting that five-year-old in charge.

Monica: I think you helped me to see one of my false beliefs just now, which is that I can't manifest anything. I think that's because when I was little and I wanted to create things, I didn't have the support to make it happen.

Dr. Margaret: But you're not five. And of course you have the support now. You have your higher self, like we all do.

Monica: The shift to the wounded self feels very subtle like it can just take over.

Dr. Margaret: It's not subtle at all. If you're depressed, you're in your wounded self. When we're connected and we're with our guidance, there is no depression unless, say, you're eating a lot of sugar and creating toxicity in the brain. I don't think that's what you're doing. I think that you've put your five-year-old in charge and you're scaring yourself. You're scaring your little girl, telling her that, "We're getting older, and we're all alone." You're scaring her and making yourself feel depressed, so you can't manifest. I can feel that you have the ability to do this, but you're going to really have to pay attention to staying connected with your guidance.

At five, you were powerless over your parents and over yourself because, when we're young, we don't have much power. Today you're still powerless over others, but not over *you*. That's the difference. Saying you're powerless now to manifest is a big lie.

Feeling powerless over others is an existential feeling of life. It's just a reality: We're helpless over others. But the good news is, you're not helpless over *you*. Right?

Monica: Right.

Dr. Margaret: How are you feeling right now?

Monica: I feel a shift. It's like the neurological hold of the wounded self on me is very strong. I've been practicing by myself to shift it, but working with you is much more powerful and immediate. When I've tried to do it myself, I just go blank. So the mirroring that you're giving me feels really important.

Dr. Margaret: That's also because I come to you with my own higher frequency, and then you match that. We have mirror neurons that can match another's frequency.

Monica: Yeah. It's like what's happening now is some of the mothering.

Dr. Margaret: That's right. Being seen, being nurtured, and it's what you need to be giving to yourself.

Monica: Thank you.

20

Healing Addictions

I want to talk about how loving yourself heals your addictions. Our addictions come from our wounded self, which wants to avoid pain. They're meant to numb us in some way, because the wounded self believes that we can't handle the existential pain of life, because as children, we couldn't. The wounded self believes that you still can't: You can't handle grief, heartbreak, loneliness, or helplessness over others, so the wounded self wants to protect you against these feelings.

The wounded self has learned many ways to avoid feelings, to numb out. It's learned to do so with various addictions, whether it's food, overeating, sugar, processed foods, alcohol, or drugs, or whether it's process addictions such as overwork, watching a lot of television, social media, video games, pornography, sex, or gambling.

Other tactics of the wounded self include judging yourself. You might feel shame, which the wounded self would rather feel than allow yourself to feel the existential pain of life. There are many other ways of abandoning, ignoring, and making others responsible. Addictions are meant to avoid your pain. That's what they're about.

Nonetheless, the pain is letting you know that you're abandoning yourself or that something is happening externally that needs your attention. In short, you're avoiding your roadmaps for what you need in order to love yourself. This is what the wounded self is always going to do the minute there's a hint of some pain, whether it's anxiety, depression, guilt, shame, anger, loneliness, emptiness, heartbreak, or helplessness. The wounded self does not want to feel these feelings and does not want to learn from them, so it will numb them out.

As you practice Inner Bonding, you learn to show up for your feelings, which is part of learning to love yourself, just as a child wants you to attend to his or her feelings. As you learn more and more about loving yourself, you learn from all your feelings. You learn to be in your body. You learn to know when you're feeling peaceful and full of love inside and when you're not. Learning to do that will keep you from turning to addictions.

People think it's hard to heal addictions. Sometimes it is very hard, because circumstances can make life really challenging. If you don't know how to manage the feelings, you're going to numb yourself out, so there's no way to move beyond addiction. But I hope you can see that if you learn to love yourself, you don't need the addictions; you don't need to numb out; you don't need to avoid. You become a fuller and much more vibrant person.

Joy and pain exist in the same place in the heart, so if you're avoiding your pain, you are not going to end up filled with joy. If you're avoiding your pain, it means that you're abandoning yourself, you're not loving yourself. You're not filling yourself with love, so you're not getting the greatest joy in life, which is sharing love. You can have this with anybody that you're open to. It doesn't even have to be a partner, a family member, or a close friend. Any interaction can be fulfilling and satisfying when you're open to sharing love, and the other person is too.

The way to resolve addictions is learning to love yourself, which means being okay with being in pain rather than avoiding it. Addictions are about avoiding pain. That is how we learned to manage pain when we were growing up, because we couldn't handle it. We got addicted to dissociating and numbing out in many ways—and those are addictions.

Many people are addicted to anger—going after somebody else to avoid their pain—because that's what they saw in their families. They saw somebody using anger and blame to avoid their pain. Those are addictions too. Anything that is used to avoid your pain is an addiction. I love to read, but I don't read to avoid my pain. I read because I love to read. If every time I was in pain, I went and got a book, I'd be using reading as an addiction to avoid pain.

People can use sleep as a way to avoid pain. Of course, we all need to sleep. Sleep is generally not an addiction, but if you use sleep to avoid your pain, then it, too, becomes an addictive way to avoid your pain.

Inner Bonding is a process for learning to learn from and lovingly manage your pain and learning to love yourself. As you learn to love yourself, the addictions will naturally fall away. You won't want them; you won't want to avoid your feelings. You will want your feelings in order to learn, and you will know how to manage them, so there's no reason to avoid them.

I've seen over and over with my clients that as they learn and practice Inner Bonding, their addictions naturally fall away. It's not like you have to white-knuckle it (although with some substances, like nicotine, there might be some white-knuckling). I used to be addicted to sugar. I was a sugar addict, and I would use sugar to avoid my pain all the time. But as I learned and practiced Inner Bonding, that addiction fell away. I was using sugar to numb out.

With Inner Bonding, that addiction just went away. It was amazing. I never would have thought it would happen because I was so addicted, but it did. I don't even like sugar anymore. I never would have thought I would reach that place. I was also addicted to anger and caretaking. Those are not there for me anymore. They fell away when I learned to love myself.

If you have addictions that you don't want, instead of focusing on the addiction, focus on Inner Bonding; focus on learning to love yourself. You will be amazed at what happens with addictions.

Mental Gymnastics

Maria: A couple months ago, I had a session with you, and you were telling me how my path is to heal the core pain and to stop judging myself for it. I've been working with that. I was always avoiding it with addictions, but I'm not using them anymore.

But today I feel lonely, I feel heartbreak, and I feel grief. And I cry. I'm going through so many processes with all this. Today I feel all this anger come up, and I think it might be my wounded self. I'm sick of this, because if I'm not using some addictive behavior, like calling a friend or eating something to avoid, I have all these bad feelings. A part of me is saying, "I'm so sick of this. How long are we going to feel bad?" I cried so much today. I've had some really beautiful healings with my little girl, but I just feel angry right now.

Dr. Margaret: So take some deep breaths into both the anger and the feelings that you are sick of feeling. What's happening inside right now?

Maria: My lips are shaking.

Dr. Margaret: What's happening in your gut and your chest?

Maria: I feel like I can start crying again.

Dr. Margaret: It's sad. So there's sadness, a lot of sadness, and there's anger about the fact that you keep on feeling this. Is that right?

Maria: Yeah. Because it keeps going on and on.

Dr. Margaret: I want you to breathe into the sadness, the feeling of wanting to cry, and make a decision that you want responsibility for that. Breathe into your heart, open to learning, and invite the love and compassion and strength and wisdom and courage and truth of spirit into your heart.

I'd like you to ask that sad little girl if there's anything that you are doing, anything you're telling her, any way you're treating her, anything you're not doing that's making her feel sad. Then go inside to the sadness. What does your little girl want to say to you?

Maria: She said, "I just want to have fun."

Dr. Margaret: Ask her what you're doing that's stopping her from having fun.

Maria: Brooding all the time.

Dr. Margaret: So you're brooding, and your little girl is not having any fun. Let's go a little deeper into the wounded self and ask the wounded self about it. There must be a good reason that she's brooding.

Maria: The wounded self says, "I have to worry about everything."

Dr. Margaret: "I have to worry about everything." There must be a good reason that she has to brood and worry about everything.

Maria: To make sure everything's okay.

Dr. Margaret: So the wounded self says, "If I brood and worry about everything, I can have control over everything being okay." Is that right?

Maria: I think so.

Dr. Margaret: The wounded self is in charge, and she's brooding and trying to control and make sure that everything's okay. That's an intention to control.

Maria: I think I'm getting all confused.

Dr. Margaret: This is not existential pain. This is a mistake that people sometimes make. If it were the existential pain, you wouldn't be feeling so bad; it would move through. It does move through fairly quickly.

Maria: I've had experiences like that.

Dr. Margaret: This sadness is not coming from existential pain. It's coming from the fact that the wounded self is in charge, trying to control, worrying, brooding, imagining that she can think of everything ahead of time and make sure everything's okay. Is that right?

Maria: I think so.

Dr. Margaret: Now let's move into step four. Imagine yourself in a beautiful place in nature at a picnic table with your higher guidance. I want you to ask, "Can my young or adolescent wounded self have control over future things by brooding and worrying?" What's happening?

Maria: I'm hearing my higher self say that I'm feeling so bad because my wounded self is trying to control everything.

Dr. Margaret: Yes, that's right. The wounded self is trying to control everything. Ask your guidance, does the wounded self have control? She thinks she does, but does she actually have control over everything?

Maria: No.

Dr. Margaret: Ask your guidance, what would be loving to you instead of worrying and brooding and not having any fun?

Maria: She's saying, "Just put your arms around yourself and be okay with whatever's happening."

Dr. Margaret: What's happening right now?

Maria: Today I saw my ex and his new partner—I hadn't seen them for about six weeks—and it sent me into a huge downward spiral again. I do so much work around it, and I think the angry part is saying, "I'm sick of this. I'm sick of trying to work through this with all these mental gymnastics and all this Inner Bonding. I'm just tired of it."

Dr. Margaret: So your little girl is tired of your wounded self trying to control everything, and she's angry at you for putting your wounded self in charge, trying to control everything rather than focusing on what's loving to you. Ask your guidance, "What would be loving to me right now? What does my little girl need from me right now?"

Maria: She's saying to put my arms around myself, put a circle of acceptance around everything, and know it'll pass after some time.

Dr. Margaret: If you were to do something fun today or tomorrow, what would it be?

Maria: The first thing I heard is jumping and playing and dancing.

Dr. Margaret: It sounds like that's what your little girl wants.

Maria: I painted tonight. I was trying to do something fun, but I was brooding during it.

Dr. Margaret: Just realize that you're feeling bad because your wounded self is in charge, brooding and worrying, trying to control something that you have no control over, and your little girl is very sad and feels abandoned by that.

Maria: I think I am getting so confused because I'm trying to not abandon her and doing all this work, but it's turning into mental gymnastics and confusion.

Dr. Margaret: You're doing Inner Bonding, but it's your wounded self who's doing it. If you were really doing Inner Bonding, you would not be crying or miserable. You would be doing something loving for yourself. So whatever you're doing isn't Inner Bonding; it's from the wounded self.

Maria: Yeah. I think I need to maybe go outside and walk in a fresh environment.

Dr. Margaret: That sounds like a really good idea.

Epilogue

I hope you have enjoyed and benefited from this brief experience of the astonishing power of Inner Bonding. And I hope you are motivated to learn and practice this powerful process and make it a part of your everyday life. Everything changes for the better when you learn to stop abandoning yourself with your self-judgments, with ignoring your feelings, with numbing with various addictions, and with making others responsible for your feelings.

Life becomes an ever-evolving experience of deepening your ability to love yourself and share your love with others, and of your ability to express and manifest your gifts in the world. Relationships flourish because becoming able to share love rather than trying to control getting love is one of the beautiful results of practicing Inner Bonding.

And I hope I see you in my masterclass!

About the Author

DR. MARGARET PAUL is the cocreator of Inner Bonding®, along with Dr. Erika Chopich, and is author/coauthor of several best-selling books, including *Do I Have to Give Up Me to Be Loved by You?*; *Do I Have to Give Up Me to Be Loved By You?: The Workbook*; *Inner Bonding*; *Healing Your Aloneness*; *The Healing Your Aloneness Workbook*; *Do I Have to Give Up Me to Be Loved by My Kids?*; *Do I Have to Give Up Me to Be Loved by God?*; *Diet for Divine Connection: Beyond Junk Foods and Junk Thoughts to At-Will Spiritual Connection*; *The Inner Bonding Workbook: Six Steps to Healing Yourself and Connecting with Your Divine Guidance*, and *Six Steps to Total Self-Healing: The Inner Bonding Process*.

Dr. Paul's books have been distributed around the world and have been translated into many languages. She holds a PhD in psychology and is a relationship expert, noted public speaker, workshop leader, educator, consultant, and artist. She has appeared on many radio and TV shows, including *The Oprah*

Show. She has successfully worked with tens of thousands of individuals, couples, and business relationships and has taught classes and seminars since 1967.

Margaret continues to work with individuals, couples, and groups throughout the world on the phone, Zoom, and Skype. During her sessions, workshops, and Intensives, she is able to access her own and her clients' spiritual guidance, which enables her to work with people wherever they are in the world. She offers life-changing thirty-day courses, and she continues to conduct One-Day Inner Bonding Breakthroughs, Inner Bonding Workshops and Three-Day and Five-Day Inner Bonding intensives. She continues to develop content for www.innerbonding.com, and her passion is distributing Self-Quest®, the online program that teaches Inner Bonding. It is being offered to prisons and schools and sold to the general public.

In her spare time, Margaret loves to paint, make pottery, read, learn, grow, and spend time with her loved ones.

www.ingramcontent.com/pod-product-compliance
Ingram Content Group UK Ltd.
Pitfield, Milton Keynes, MK11 3LW, UK
UKHW021311180426
11947UKWH00015B/1169